Derrida's *Of Grammatology*

Edinburgh Philosophical Guides Series

Derrida's *Of Grammatology*

An Edinburgh Philosophical Guide

Arthur Bradley

Edinburgh University Press

Edinburgh University Press Ltd
22 George Square, Edinburgh

Typeset in 11/13pt Monotype Baskerville by
Servis Filmsetting Ltd, Manchester, and
printed and bound by Antony Rowe Ltd, Chippenham, Wilts

A CIP record for this book is available from the British Library

ISBN 978 0 7486 2612 0 (hardback)
ISBN 978 0 7486 2613 7 (paperback)

Contents

Series Editor's Preface

To us, the principle of this series of books is clear and simple: what readers new to philosophical classics need first and foremost is help with *reading* these key texts. That is to say, help with the often antique or artificial style, the twists and turns of arguments on the page, as well as the vocabulary found in many philosophical works. New readers also need help with those first few daunting and disorienting sections of these books, the point of which are not at all obvious. The books in this series take you through each text step-by-step, explaining complex key terms and difficult passages which help to illustrate the way a philosopher thinks in prose.

We have designed each volume in the series to correspond to the way the texts are actually taught at universities around the world, and have included helpful guidance on writing university-level essays or examination answers. Designed to be read alongside the text, our aim is to enable you to *read* philosophical texts with confidence and perception. This will enable you to make your own judgements on the texts, and on the variety of opinions to be found concerning them. We want you to feel able to join the great dialogue of philosophy, rather than remain a well-informed eavesdropper.

Douglas Burnham

Acknowledgements

I am very grateful to the many friends and colleagues who helped in all manner of ways during the process of writing this book: Louis Armand, Simon Bainbridge, Brian Baker, Fred Botting, Mick Dillon, Paul Fletcher, Mike Greaney, Will Large, Lindsey Moore, Lynne Pearce, John Schad, Andy Tate and Jim Urpeth. Particular thanks must go to my students in the Department of English and Creative Writing at Lancaster University, on whom much of this material was originally tested.

I would also like to thank Douglas Burnham, the series editor, for inviting me to write this volume in the first place, together with Carol McDonald and the editorial team at Edinburgh University Press for guiding the manuscript through to publication.

I am more grateful than I can say to Rebecca Smith and to my parents, Anne and John Bradley, for all their support over the years.

Finally, I would like to thank Abir Hamdar for reading and commenting on every chapter of this book and for everything that has happened since: *inti habibti* Abir.

Note on Texts

This book refers to Gayatri Chakravorty Spivak's English translation of Jacques Derrida's *Of Grammatology* in the first instance, because this is the version of the text that the vast majority of anglophone readers will be using. However, I follow each reference to the English translation with the corresponding reference to the original French text, so that interested readers may chase this up if they so wish. In general, then, page references to Derrida's text will take the following form: *Grammatology*, p. 214/308.

Introduction

Jacques Derrida is now generally agreed – by both devotees and critics alike – to be one of the most influential philosophers of the later twentieth century. He was born in French colonial Algeria in 1930. After completing his secondary education, Derrida moved from Algeria to France in his early twenties to study philosophy at the prestigious École Normale Supérieure in Paris. To begin with, Derrida's particular research specialism was in the field of phenomenology and he began a doctoral thesis on the work of the great phenomenologist Edmund Husserl in 1957 only to abandon it some years later. The young Derrida published a prize-winning introduction to, and translation of, Husserl in 1962 and went on to write a series of essays and reviews in French journals such as *Critique* and *Tel Quel* (1965–6). This growing body of work throughout the 1960s largely took the form of an exploration of the role played by writing (*l'écriture*) in the history of western philosophy from Plato all the way up to more contemporary figures such as Husserl. In this way, Derrida was laying the groundwork for his first major publications.

It was in 1967 that Derrida definitively entered the philosophical stage with the publication of a celebrated triptych of works that gathered together, and expanded upon, his own specialised account of 'writing': a study of Husserl's phenomenology entitled *La voix et le phénomene* (*Speech and Phenomena*), a collection of essays on contemporary figures such as Claude Lévi-Strauss, Michel Foucault and Emmanuel Levinas called *L'écriture et la différence* (*Writing and Difference*) and, perhaps most famously of all, a study of the 'science' of writing itself, which went under the name of *De la grammatologie*.[1] As a result of these and subsequent works like *La Dissémination* (*Dissemination*) (1972) and *Marges de la philosophie* (*Margins of Philosophy*) (1972),

Derrida's reputation as a philosopher grew to international proportions. The translation of many of his early works in the 1970s brought Derrida's work to the attention of the anglophone world for the first time. This increasingly global profile led Derrida to divide his professional life between institutions in France (the École Normale Supérieure, the École des Hautes Études en Sciences Sociales) and a series of prestigious appointments in the USA (Yale University, the University of California at Irvine).

To put it simply, Jacques Derrida became not just one of the best-known names in contemporary philosophy in the 1970s and 1980s but something of a media phenomenon whose fame stretched far beyond the walls of the university. His mode of philosophy – which quickly acquired the famous or notorious brand name of 'deconstruction' – has influenced almost every academic discipline from art history to zoology. It has even caught the popular imagination: Derrida himself has been the subject of several films and at least one pop song, whereas 'deconstruction' has become the name of everything from a style of architecture to a record label. If comparatively few people have read such large and formidably difficult tomes as *De la grammatologie* – whether in the French original or the English translation – it often seems that absolutely everybody has heard of Derrida and has an opinion about his thought. In the forty years since the *Grammatologie* was first published, Derrida's deconstruction has been variously celebrated and castigated as everything from a kind of intellectual terrorism that seeks to destroy everything western culture holds dear to a liberatory politics of difference, freedom or personal choice.

For Derrida, however, his early explorations of the problem of 'writing' in western thought only represented the beginning of a much wider enquiry and his many subsequent texts develop this theme in new, singular and surprising directions. After the 1960s, he went on to explore such diverse areas, themes and disciplines as art and architecture, literature, linguistics, politics and international relations, psychoanalysis, religious studies and theology, technology and the media, and witnessing and testimony. From the 1980s onwards, it also becomes possible to detect an increasingly marked 'ethical' or 'political' turn in Derrida's work and thought. The philosopher at least appears to move away from the seemingly 'abstract' philosophical questions of the earlier work and to gravitate towards 'concrete' political problems such as apartheid, the fall of communism and the future of Europe. This impression is confirmed by the appearance of an increasingly ethical – even theological – vocabulary in the later work which draws on such themes as the gift, sacrifice, the impossible, and perhaps most intriguingly, the messianic. In October 2004, Jacques Derrida died at the age of seventy-four.

Of Grammatology

It is with *De la grammatologie* – which was published in English translation as *Of Grammatology* in 1976 – that most anglophone readers encounter Derrida for the first time.[2] As we have already suggested, the *Grammatology* is Derrida best-known work but it remains a forbidding challenge for any reader: the book's single most famous line – '*there is no outside-text* ['*il n'y a pas de hors-texte*']' (*Grammatology*, p. 158/227) – is regularly mistranslated, misquoted or simply misunderstood even today. To put it bluntly, Derrida is *difficult*: his philosophical style is often deeply idiosyncratic and challenges formal or argumentative norms in a way that, for new and experienced readers alike, can sometimes seem almost wilfully perverse. Yet, the main reasons why the *Grammatology* is, for all its fame, somewhat under-read are, in fact, quite straightforward. First, Derrida's text arises out of a very specific intellectual climate that may well seem daunting to the modern reader. On the one hand, it presupposes a knowledge of a certain philosophical tradition (Hegel, Nietzsche, Husserl and Heidegger). On the other, it engages with what in France are called the 'human sciences' (linguistics, psychoanalysis, anthropology) and the then-dominant intellectual movement called 'structuralism'. Second, and more importantly, however, Derrida's *own* philosophy proceeds – in stark contrast to his reputation as a master 'theorist' who deals in grand, abstract claims – via a series of minutely detailed, almost claustrophobic, readings of texts. If we want to follow his argument in the detail it requires, it is necessary to have a close familiarity with the work of the eighteenth-century philosopher Jean-Jacques Rousseau, the linguist Ferdinand de Saussure and the anthropologist Claude Lévi-Strauss: what Derrida has to say always emerges *through* the received ideas, concepts and vocabulary of his host texts and it is this almost forensic submersion that gives rise to the common allegations of obscurantism. For Derrida, what has become known as 'deconstruction' is not a 'theory' in the traditional sense of a general set of rules that can be applied to particular cases, but rather something that always takes place *within*, and cannot be separated from, the singular texts he is reading.

As this book will make clear, however, there is another, even more important, reason why *Of Grammatology* poses such a challenge to new readers and this is not so much a question of its historical context or its own unique style as its *argument*. It is what Derrida's book has to say – as opposed to the supposedly obscurantist way in which he says it – that is the most formidable obstacle to anyone approaching his work for the first time. Quite simply, Derrida puts into question everything – meaning, language, interpretation, authorial intention, even the idea of the book as a fixed or finite repository of meaning with a beginning and an end – that we think we know about the process of 'reading' itself. If we all tend to bring certain assumptions to the reading process about what, how and why we read – even something as basic as the idea that we read in order to find out what an author has to say to us or what a book means – what Derrida's book seeks to analyse, and place in historical context, is *why* we have these preconceptions in the first place: '[i]n what you call my books' he once told an interviewer, 'what is first of all put in question is the unity of the book and the unity "book" considered as a perfect totality' (*Positions*, p. 3). The everyday or common-sense ideas we have about reading rely, whether we know it or not, on a deep-rooted philosophical tradition that Derrida spends the whole of the *Grammatology* seeking to call into question. This is not to say that such ideas are simply wrong – an enduring misconception of Derrida's work is that he does not believe in truth, meaning or authorial intentionality at all – but they are anything but a 'natural' or 'objective' reflection of 'the way things are'. In this sense, Derrida's philosophy ultimately forces us to ask important questions about what we mean by 'meaning' itself and the answers he supplies are often radically counter-intuitive.

The Argument

To begin with, then, I want to offer a very brief outline of the subject matter of the *Grammatology* as a point of orientation for the rest of this book. It is important to recognise from the very outset that – for all his alleged attempts to question truth, meaning or authority – Derrida's philosophy stands or falls on the quality of its argument. As we have already suggested, this argument is challenging and often difficult to follow, but it is indisputably *there* and we can trace its progression through a series of interlinked steps. Let me set these out in turn:

1. First, Derrida's book is self-evidently a study of something called 'grammatology' – but what exactly does this obscure word mean? As its intriguing etymology makes clear, 'grammatology' quite literally means 'writing talk' (*gramme-logy*) and this somewhat paradoxical idea of *speaking* about *writing* is, we will see later on, very revealing. It is more common, however, to say that the term refers to the *science* of writing in the same way that, say, 'biology' is the scientific study of living things: grammatology, properly understood, is the study of what writing is, when and how it originated, and the ways in which it differs from other forms of communication like speech. For Derrida, the study of writing goes as far back as Plato but, strictly speaking, the science of 'grammatology' itself is a more modern one. In the 'Exergue' to the book, he makes clear that his own work on writing is only a small part of a much wider revolution in modern thought that seeks to use writing as an explanatory model for developments in the fields of linguistics, psychoanalysis, molecular biology and cybernetics (*Grammatology*, p. 4/13).

2. It is important to recognise a crucial ambiguity in the title of Derrida's book, however. As he goes on to make clear, this book may well be *about* grammatology but it is not *itself* actually a science of writing: '*Of Grammatology*' he told a contemporary interviewer, 'is not a defence and illustration of grammatology' (*Positions* p. 12). On the contrary, it is important to hear a silent question mark in the title of the book:

Of Grammatology is the title of a question: a question about the necessity of a science of writing, about the conditions that would make it possible, about the critical work that would have to open its field and resolve the epistemological obstacles. (*Positions*, p. 13)

For Derrida, in other words, grammatology is the site of a problem rather than a solution and it raises a whole series of larger questions –

about writing, about speech, about the nature of science and even of truth itself – that will be the main subject of his work. In fact, Derrida even goes so far as to say that this new 'science' of writing – grammatology itself – might, strictly speaking, be impossible: 'a science of writing runs the risk of never being established as such and with that name' (*Grammatology* p. 4/13). Why might this be?

3. As we will see, it is now that Derrida's apparently modest argument begins to reveal the true vastness of its ambition. To introduce the first key premise of his thought more generally, Derrida argues that 'grammatology' offers us an insight into a much bigger set of philosophical assumptions, namely, the 'metaphysics of presence [la métaphysique de la présence]' (p. 49/71). What exactly does this forbidding term mean? It is generally understood that 'metaphysics' is the name for a specific branch of philosophy that seeks to locate an ultimate ground, essence or foundation of reality that lies beyond the physical or empirical world: the classic example of such a position would be Plato's idealism which argues that our world is merely the imitation of a pre-existing world of permanent, unchanging Ideas or Forms. However, Derrida has a much more ambitious understanding of 'metaphysics' that encompasses the entire history of western philosophy from Plato to the present day. For Derrida, the western philosophical tradition in its entirety can be described as 'metaphysical' in the sense that it all seeks to establish an essential foundation for reality and, in his view, that foundation is something called 'presence'. If western philosophy has developed in many different directions over the last 2,500 years, what all these movements have in common is an attempt to posit a full or pure 'presence' as the supreme value by which all reality can be judged. From the spatial presence of something we can see, hear or touch, through the temporal presence of the 'here and now' in which we live, up to and including the *absence* of some presence that has been lost (such as an Edenic state of nature) or which may be achieved in the future (such as the return of God), western thought consistently comes to the same conclusion: *what is most real, true or important is what is most present*. In Derrida's view, the 'metaphysics of presence' historically operates by erecting a series of binary oppositions between concepts, values or terms where, in each case, one concept is identified as the bearer of presence itself whereas the other is identified with the falling away, or loss of, that presence:

the transcendental is privileged as more 'present' than the empirical, the ideal is championed over the material, the soul over the body, the masculine over the feminine and so on *ad infinitum*.

4. To introduce what is perhaps the single most important feature of his philosophy more generally, Derrida argues that this metaphysical concept of 'presence' relies on a grounding or foundational *instability*: it is not as simple or straightforward as it seems. It is this critique of 'presence' that lies in the background of the *Grammatology* even if it is not always explicit in the text itself. As strange or counter-intuitive as it may seem at this early stage, whatever we perceive or experience as fully 'present' – the sound of my own voice, the wooden desk that I can touch in front of me, the thoughts that are running through my head while I read or write, even the 'here and now' of space and time in which I exist – is actually shot through with an infinite, and almost imperceptible, number of differences, delays or spaces. Quite simply, Derrida argues that every apparently pure, stable or self-identical presence is nothing more than an effect generated by a prior series of differences: nothing is ever purely or simply 'there'. If the metaphysics of presence often presents itself as scientific, neutral or simply 'the way things are', its binary logic of oppositions and hierarchies is the product of a very questionable series of decisions: why, for example, has the masculine been historically deemed to be *more* real, present or authentic more than the feminine? For Derrida, as we will see, the 'deconstruction' of western metaphysics consists in a patient interrogation or testing of this oppositional logic: what begin as a series of mutually antagonistic oppositions and hierarchies – masculinity versus femininity – can be shown to unravel into a mutually defining or dependent network of differences. In every case, Derrida shows that the supposedly primary, dominant or superior value implicitly relies on the supposedly secondary, different or inferior value in order to achieve the presence that it should achieve all by itself: the masculine depends upon the feminine in order to define its own identity in the first place. What form does this process take in the *Grammatology*?

5. For Derrida, *Of Grammatology* takes the form of an extended analysis of the metaphysical opposition between *speech* and *writing*. It focuses on what the philosopher takes to be a defining form of what we have called the metaphysical search for 'presence': *logocentrism* (p. 3/11). According to the etymology of the term, 'logocentrism'

signifies the philosophical attempt to find what the Ancient Greeks called the *logos*: a term which can be literally translated as 'word' but also carries within it the larger sense of 'logic', 'reason' or 'meaning'. Yet, what characterises this particular metaphysical attempt to establish a present ground, essence or foundation, Derrida argues, is that it does so through the means of *speech* (p. 3/11). To pave the way for another key move in his argument, Derrida contends that logocentrism prioritises speech (*phone*) over writing (*gramme*) as the original or privileged means by which the presence of the *logos* is expressed. Why, though, does logocentrism champion speech over writing? On the one hand, speech is believed to be the most pure and immediate expression of the thought, intentions or 'presence' of the speaker: I am always 'there' or present when I speak to someone, for example, and my intentions are communicated directly to them without any need of an aid or intermediary. On the other hand, however, writing is deemed to be at best a mediation and at worst a corruption of the pure presence of speech: I am obviously not present as you read this book, for instance, because it possesses a 'life of its own' which enables it to be read quite independently of me and even my intentions. To consider the status of writing from the perspective of logocentrism is to confront something that is essentially 'phonetic' in origin, that is to say, inferior to, or derivative of, speech (p. 3/11). For Derrida, this logocentric account of the relation between speech and writing dominates not simply the study of writing, but western philosophy more generally: western thought regularly denounces writing in the most extreme or violent terms as base, empty and (precisely because it can function in the absence of the author) untrustworthy or open to misinterpretation. In Derrida's account, the story of western thought from Plato up to the science of grammatology or 'writing talk' itself – with all the ideas, concepts and traditions it contains – might even be said to be the story of the 'debasement of writing, and its repression outside "full" speech' (p. 3/12).

6. Now, this oppositional account of the relationship between speech and writing is, if everything we have said about the instability of the metaphysical tradition holds true, a very problematic one. It is Derrida's contention that this tradition is not an innocent, objective description of 'the way things really are', remember, but a set of complex, questionable assumptions that are the products of a very

particular time and place: logocentrism might even be described as the most 'original and powerful ethnocentrism', he writes in the 'Exergue', because it violently privileges and imposes the values of western culture over all others (p. 3/12). As we have already hinted, Derrida has his own specialised idea of 'writing' and this concept goes far beyond the traditional, logocentric understanding of the term as a mere set of empirical marks (like the inscriptions on this page) that are, at best, an inferior substitute for the spoken word. To raise what will be the single largest, controversial and far-reaching argument in the *Grammatology*, Derrida challenges the logocentric attempt to champion speech over writing by arguing that *all* language – whether spoken or written – might be described as 'writing': *writing is another name for language itself*. However, what exactly does this remarkable, even shocking, claim actually mean? We need to be careful to clarify precisely what Derrida is saying here because – in many ways – the entire *Grammatology* rests on this argument. To say that all language is writing is not to make a dubious historical claim about the chrono-logical priority of the written word (p. 323n/17n) – as if Derrida really believed that writing preceded speech or literate culture came before oral culture – so much as to advance a more subtle philosoph-ical or conceptual claim about the nature of language as such. For Derrida, as we will see, what this claim actually means is that all lan-guage is characterised by that quality of *mediation* that the logocentric tradition historically attributes to 'writing' alone. If the logocentric account of writing tends to presume that writing comes on to the scene in order to filter the pure expression of speech, Derrida will suggest that this state of mediation is the original condition of all language including the – supposedly ideal – spoken word. In the *Grammatology*, this so-called 'originary writing [*arche-écriture*]' (p. 56/83) becomes the basis of an entirely new philosophy of language but, as we will see, it also says something very important about our experi-ence of the 'real world' beyond language too.

7. Finally, then, and to go back to where we started, we can now perhaps begin to glimpse *why* Derrida chooses to focus his argument around the – apparently – marginal and obscure topic of 'gramma-tology'. It is Derrida's hypothesis that the marginalisation of writing in western thought is not simply 'wrong', an accident or a meaning-less event. On the contrary, it is a privileged symptom of a much

larger metaphysical prejudice in favour of an essentially fixed, simple or 'present' meaning that goes far beyond the comparatively limited question of language itself to encompass everything we understand by 'reality' per se. To put it another way, Derrida's *Grammatology* is nothing less than a fundamental re-evaluation of the basic tenets of western thinking: what it understands as truth and falsehood, what it champions and what it excludes, what it assumes and what it represses or denies. However, it is very important to add one note of caution before we go any further: Derrida does not propose that we can ever simply *overcome* logocentric or metaphysical assumptions. We cannot simply establish some new, more accurate theory or system of knowledge to replace the metaphysics of presence (*Positions*, p. 12). If Derrida's work is a thoroughgoing interrogation of metaphysics, the fact remains that he is deeply sceptical of any attempt to get 'beyond' it for the very simple reason that we have no way of thinking, talking or writing that is not dominated by the metaphysical tradition: '[w]e have no language – no syntax and no lexicon – which is foreign to this history' he writes in a contemporaneous essay.[3] To reject metaphysics *tout court*, in other words, is to reject language and thought itself. For Derrida, as we will see throughout this book, any attempt to simply escape logocentrism merely leads to the establishment of some new *logos* or pure, unmediated centre of meaning and, as a result, we end up right back where we started: we thus have no alternative but to use and embrace the very concepts – 'speech', 'writing' etc. – that we wish to call into question.[4] In other words, Derrida's challenge is to articulate a way of reading that does not remain faithfully inside the logocentric tradition nor pretends that one can simply move outside it, but rather shows (in a paradoxical sense that will have to defined carefully) the instability or contingency of that tradition from *within*: 'The movements of deconstruction do not destroy structures from the outside. They are not possible and effective, nor can they take accurate aim, except by inhabiting those structures' (*Grammatology*, p. 24/39).

Conclusion

In *Derrida's* Of Grammatology: *An Edinburgh Philosophical Guide*, I will provide a introduction to this key contemporary text that hopefully provides new readers with everything they need to approach the *Grammatology* for the first time. First, Chapter 1 offers an introduction to the philosophical context of Derrida's philosophy and, in particular, his critique of phenomenology and structuralism. After examining the historical origins of the text, Chapter 2 moves on to give a chapter-by-chapter commentary upon the work itself. To begin with, we will analyse Derrida's examination of the 'science of writing'. We will then turn to Derrida's reading of the work of the linguist Ferdinand de Saussure and, in particular, his attempt to articulate the concept of an 'originary' trace or writing. The next section concerns the philosopher's account of the anthropologist Claude Lévi-Strauss and, more generally, the relationship between writing and violence. This discussion is followed by a more general and schematic look at Derrida's analysis of perhaps the single most important figure in the *Grammatology*: Jean-Jacques Rousseau. Finally, Study Aids offers a glossary of terms, a summary of influential readings of the text and some tips on answering essay and examination questions in order to help new readers get to grips with some of the larger issues that are at stake in Derrida's text.

The following book is, however, still only a *guide* to Derrida's *Of Grammatology*. It is not possible to offer a complete commentary upon the whole text in the space available. Accordingly, this book should definitely not be seen as a substitute for reading the *Grammatology* itself. However, if everything Derrida claims is true, then there is a much more important reason why a book like this one cannot do justice to his work. To put it bluntly, Derrida's text calls into question the logocentric agenda that lie behind the activity of 'reading' itself and the problem is that this book is – by necessity – *also* the product of these very assumptions. First, what follows almost inevitably presupposes that we can identify an original *logos*, sense or meaning within the written text that is nothing less than the one true voice (*phone*) of the historical author himself: Jacques Derrida speaks. More generally, this premise carries with it a whole series of other assumptions about what Derrida is saying and what he is not, which ideas are important and which are not, which historical and philosophical contexts we need to know about and which we do not. If there is nothing inherently wrong about any of this – Derrida's text *does* involve a series of compelling ideas which it is perfectly possible to read, understand and debate – we will have understood nothing about his work if we emerge with all our preconceived ideas about meaning intact. In this sense, there can be no reliable 'guide' to *Of Grammatology*.

This is a guide book, then, that calls into question the very possibility of a guide book. It will do its best to present Derrida's thought in a clear, simple and accessible way but, in doing so, we will continually run up against the limitations of our own ideas about reading, authorship, history, politics and even the concept of the book itself. As I have already hinted, we cannot simply recover Derrida's own original intention, meaning or purpose from the *Grammatology* without missing the entire point of the theory of language it proposes. For Derrida, all language – whether spoken or written – exists in an irreducible state of mediation: we cannot simply return to the animating intentions, consciousness or 'presence' of the user, speaker or author. From the moment we begin to speak or write, in other words, we set in motion a complex linguistic machine that has a 'life' quite independent of our own: what we call *Of Grammatology* is a cog in that mechanism. If we cannot return to the true, original or intended meaning of Derrida's text, this means that there can be no end to the process of reading, analysing and interpreting it: the meaning of the text does not lie behind us in some distant past, in other words, but in front of us, in the future, as something that is yet to be decided. In all these senses, I think the task of reading Derrida's *Of Grammatology* can only be an endless one, but let us at least begin.

Notes

1. To be sure, Derrida's first three major publications are deeply intertwined with one another and it is somewhat artificial to consider them in isolation. As Derrida himself says 'One can take *Of Grammatology* as a long essay articulated in two parts . . . into the middle of which one could staple *Writing and Difference*. *Grammatology* often calls upon it'. In the same way, he says of *Speech and Phenomena*: 'I could have bound it as a long note to one or the other of the other two works. *Of Grammatology* refers to it and economises its development'. See Jacques Derrida, *Positions*, trans. Alan Bass (Chicago: University of Chicago Press, 1981), pp. 4–5. All further references will be abbreviated in the text.

2. Jacques Derrida, *Of Grammatology*, trans. Gayatri Chakravrorty Spivak (Baltimore, MD, and London: Johns Hopkins University Press, 1976). All further references will be abbreviated in the text.

3. Jacques Derrida, 'Structure, Sign and Play in the Discourse of the Human Sciences' in *Writing and Difference*, trans. Alan Bass (Routledge & Kegan Paul, 1978), pp. 278–95, esp. 280. All further references will be abbreviated in the text.

4. In Derrida's account, any attempt to simply or dogmatically *invert* the assumptions of metaphysics – as many anti-metaphysical philosophers do, for example, when they try to argue the body is *more* present than the soul, the empirical *more* present than the transcendental and so on – still remains rooted within the logic of binary oppositions and the illusion of total presence (*Grammatology*, p. 19, 315/32, 444).

1. Historical Context

Jacques Derrida's *Of Grammatology* (1967) is now old enough to belong to the history of philosophy. It is thus important to begin our study of it by trying to understand the historical, philosophical and broader intellectual context within which it was written. As we have already begun to see, Derrida's text emerged at a very specific moment in post-war continental philosophy and we cannot hope to read his work without some appreciation of the larger debates, controversies and movements that animated it. Unfortunately, this is easier said than done. To be sure, Derrida's work does not exist in some sort of timeless vacuum but, all the same, it is very difficult to locate it within a particular context, tradition or lineage. First, it is remarkable for the vast range of its historical scope: Derrida's philosophy tackles nothing less than the entire western tradition and so any analysis of it cannot hope to be exhaustive.[1] Second, however, Derrida's work is also a *critique* of that western tradition in its entirety. From Platonic idealism all the way through to Heidegger's concept of Being, western thought can be seen as the product of a metaphysical commitment to the value of *presence*. If this is the case, then Derrida's own thought cannot simply be identified with the western tradition as a whole nor with any of the various debates or schools (idealism, empiricism, materialism) of which it is comprised. Finally, however, I think there is a more fundamental reason still why we must be careful to avoid explaining the *Grammatology* with reference to its philosophical or cultural sources: the argument of the book itself. For Derrida, as we will see, the philosophical concept of 'history' itself is the product of the very metaphysical assumptions he is attempting to call into question. In this chapter I will offer a brief history of Derrida's thought up to the *Grammatology*, but we will also begin to see how his thought poses a challenge to the way in which we understand 'history' itself.

Beyond Metaphysics?

To begin with, I want to focus on the philosophical background to Derrida's critique of metaphysics. It would be quite wrong to assume that Derrida is the first thinker to question the metaphysical assumptions that lie at the core of western philosophy: the critique of metaphysics is, in many ways, as old as metaphysics itself. As we have already suggested, metaphysics is that branch of philosophy that asks the following question: 'What is the supreme ground of reality?'. First of all, of course, Plato answered this question by saying that what we call 'reality' was merely the likeness of a realm of independent and universal Forms. However, as philosophy became more and more aware of its own epistemological limits – the problem of what, if anything, we can know for sure about the world outside our own experience – metaphysics became more cautious about making strong ontological or theological claims about the nature of reality. If the essential metaphysical question still remained the same – what is? – the answer changed from 'the ideal', 'substance' or 'god' to the 'thinking or knowing subject'. For the seventeenth-century rationalist philosopher Descartes, the *ego cogito* or thinking subject provided the only firm foundation upon which knowledge could be grounded and this position is pursued and refined in different ways by such figures as Kant and Husserl.[2] The last decades of the nineteenth century, however, saw the emergence of a new, more radical critique of metaphysics in the work of such seminal figures as Marx, Nietzsche and Freud. This so-called 'hermeneutics of suspicion' is what lays the groundwork for Derrida's own attempt to question the grounding assumptions of western metaphysics (*Writing and Difference*, p. 280). In Derrida's own view, deconstruction is heavily indebted to this larger tradition of 'anti-metaphysical philosophy' but, as we will see, his philosophy remains deeply sceptical about the possibility of ever simply getting 'beyond' metaphysics.

Marx

First, I want to mention a figure who was, until recently, a comparatively neglected source for Derrida's philosophy. Karl Marx sees all our metaphysical ideas about reality as nothing more than imaginary expressions of the processes of life, nature and history. Quite simply, our view of reality is upside-down: we must understand consciousness from the perspective of life, rather than life from the perspective of consciousness.[3] According to Marx's philosophy of historical materialism, what defines 'life' in this case is not biology but *history*: being alive is not something we *are* so much as something we *do*, the way in which we work or labour, how we organise our existence socially, materially and economically (*German Ideology*, p. 48). However, if metaphysical ideas are all completely illusory, then why does anyone believe in them in the first place? To Marx's way of thinking, human beings living under capitalism have become *alienated* – divorced – from their essential nature as workers and this real alienation is expressed in idealised form by metaphysical belief systems like Christianity: the divide between man and god in Christian theology has its roots in man's division from himself.[4] For Marx, it is only by effecting a radical transformation of the economic system through the overthrow of capitalism that it will become possible to overcome the material alienation of human beings that produces the illusions of metaphysics. If it would be too much to describe Derrida as a 'Marxist' – his early work is understandably reluctant to associate itself with Soviet or Maoist state communism (see *Positions*, pp. 37–96) – later works like *Specters of Marx* (1993) make more explicit the debt he owes to the Marxian tradition.[5] In Derrida's view, Marx's attempt to expose the historical nature of apparently timeless metaphysical concepts like 'god', 'being' or 'consciousness', his exposure of a certain 'virtual' or mediated quality at the heart of what we understand as 'reality' in his analysis of the commodity (*Specters*, p. 125–76), and, most importantly, his hope for a radically transformed or emancipated future, is something that any deconstruction worthy of the name must always affirm (*Specters*, p. 89).

Nietzsche

As Derrida makes clear on a number of occasions, a second and more obvious precursor to his thought is the late-nineteenth-century German philosopher Nietzsche. Friedrich Nietzsche famously sees the production of metaphysical belief systems as an attempt to repress the dynamic processes of life itself: the 'other' world of metaphysics is the *product* of this world rather than its cause or foundation. Proposing what he calls a 'genealogy' of metaphysics, Nietzsche shows how apparently timeless, unconditioned values arise out of the very history they are supposed to explain in the first place. Quite simply, we must see concepts like 'truth', 'being' or 'consciousness' less as descriptions of 'what is' and more as misleading linguistic abstractions of a flux of historical, physiological and affective forces. For Nietzsche, metaphysics is the product of what he calls an 'ascetic ideal' that leads human beings to renounce 'this world, *our* world' in favour of '*another world*'.[6] Yet, it is impossible to reach this other world because it never existed in the first place and so humanity falls back into '*ressentiment*': a sense of permanent guilt that finds its apex in the Christian view of human existence as 'fallen'. What lies beneath the metaphysical 'will to truth' of the ascetic ideal is the 'will to power': the capacity to liberate ourselves from the pursuit of the timeless other world of 'truth', and affirm our place within, and as a product of, the endlessly creative becoming of this world. If Derrida makes clear his debt to Nietzsche throughout his early work – he regularly acknowledges the latter's critique of language, subjectivity and metaphysics[7] – he never totally endorses Nietzsche's attempt to construct an anti-metaphysical philosophy. The problem is that, once again, Derrida is very sceptical of any philosophical position that naïvely seeks to overcome, transgress or step 'outside' metaphysics because, as we have already begun to see, every such move must borrow all its resources from the very thing it is attempting to resist. This leads him to praise Nietzsche's philosophy more for the problems it raises or makes apparent – how exactly can we resist metaphysics from within? – than the answers it supplies to such questions (*Grammatology*, p. 19/31–2). In simpler terms, however, Nietzsche's legacy to Derrida is obvious: the German thinker's attempt to write a history of supposedly a-historical metaphysical values, his deep scepticism about philosophical language – whereby abstract terms like 'truth' only serve to conceal or reify the operation of complex empirical forces and events – and his attempt to posit a philosophy of force, becoming and difference over one of stasis, being and identity all re-emerge in different forms in deconstruction.

Freud

For Derrida, another major figure who anticipates deconstruction is the 'father' of psychoanalysis, Sigmund Freud (*Writing and Difference*,

p. 280). We have already seen how Descartes' account of the *Cogito* or thinking subject provided a new and apparently firm foundation for philosophy whereby consciousness is irrefutably 'present' to itself in its own act of thinking. After Nietzsche, though, what appeared to be a stable and self-identical 'I' is revealed to be the site of a flux of unconscious historical, physiological and affective forces and events. Sigmund Freud's pyschoanalysis intensifies this critique of the rational thinking or knowing subject which had become the last refuge of metaphysics in modernity: psychoanalysis 'put[s] consciousness into question in its assured certainty of itself' Derrida writes (*Margins*, p. 17). To Freud's way of thinking, what we call the rational or self-conscious 'I' is the meeting point of a range of different, competing and often unconscious forces, desires or principles: 'consciousness may be, not the most universal attribute of human processes, but only a particular fraction of them'.[8] What is ground-breaking about psychoanalysis for Derrida is precisely this insight into how apparently simple, identical and present points of origin – such as the consciousness of the subject – are actually the product of an originary and unthought network of *differences*: 'The putting into question of the authority of consciousness is first and always differential' (*Margins*, p. 18). Even so, Derrida is no simple or uncritical follower of Freud because – just as we saw in the case of Nietzsche and Marx – he continually detects the traces of a commitment to metaphysical concepts throughout Freud's corpus. If the deconstruction of metaphysics often *looks like* a psychoanalytic project – because it seeks to reveal something close to the 'unconscious' of western philosophy – Derrida argues that Freud's system nonetheless belongs in its entirety to the history of metaphysics. The psychoanalytic system may well call into question the self-presence of consciousness but it does so at the cost of turning the *unconscious* into a 'hidden, virtual, or potential self-presence'. This means that Freud risks establishing a metaphysics of the unconscious whereby our drives and instincts become a new metaphysical basis for truth (pp. 20–1). In Derrida's account, however, Freud still remains (like Nietzsche) a highly important liminal figure in the history of thought because his work frequently manages to question the foundational assumptions of metaphysics from the 'inside': Freud's persistent analogies between the structure of the psyche and the operations of an automatic writing machine, for example, offer a crucial, if never sustained, insight into the orginary state of mediation or difference of '*arche-écriture*' which will be so important to the *Grammatology* (see *Writing and Difference*, pp. 196–231).

Heidegger

Finally, however, I would argue that the single biggest influence on Derrida is the philosophy of Martin Heidegger (*Positions*, p. 9). It is with, through, and beyond Heidegger's thought that many of Derrida's most famous concepts are worked out: Derrida's 'deconstruction' is a radicalisation of Heidegger's '*destruktion*', for example, his notion of the originary 'trace' draws on a reading of Heidegger's thinking of Being, and his critique of 'the metaphysics of presence' is an extension of the Heideggerian questioning of metaphysical essentialism. As we will see later, Derrida even borrows certain Heideggerian rhetorical strategies in his attempt to resist the metaphysics of presence: Heidegger adopts a practice of crossing out key terms in his philosophy like ~~Being~~ in order to purge them of centuries of interpretive accretions or sediments and Derrida adapts this practice of writing under erasure (*sous rature*) for his own purposes (see, for example, *Grammatology*, p. 19/31). Yet, once again, I think it would be very simplistic to see Derrida as just another 'post-Heideggerian' thinker who does little more than follow the trajectory of his master's thought, without adding anything original to the mix. To quickly summarise what is a career-long engagement with the German philosopher, Derrida is once again insistent that Heidegger's critique of metaphysics – for all its originality – still remains within the metaphysical enclosure it is attempting to exceed: 'I attempt to locate in Heidegger's text . . . the signs of a belonging to metaphysics' (*Positions*, p. 10). Let me simply list a few key points of similarity and difference between the two thinkers:

1. First, Derrida suspects that Heidegger's attempt to uncover an original experience of Being 'beyond' the metaphysics of presence risks establishing a new form of metaphysics. According to Derrida, in other words, Heidegger's Being becomes simply a more secure origin or ground for knowledge: '[i]s not the quest for an *archia*

[origin] in general . . . still the "essential" operation of metaphysics?' (*Margins*, p. 63).

2. It is also important to note that Derrida's 'deconstruction' is subtly different from Heidegger's attempt to 'destroy' the ontological content of western metaphysics in order to attain a more originary encounter with Being.[9] If there are obvious similarities between the two – both attempt to question the construction of metaphysics from *within* the tradition as opposed to criticising it from some supposedly more real 'outside' – Derrida again detects a nostalgia for a lost 'presence' within Heidegger's search for the origin (*Margins*, p. 27).

3. Perhaps Derrida's greatest debt to Heidegger, however, is the rigorous and systematic fashion in which the German philosopher describes the vicious circle in which every critique of metaphysics finds itself. For Derrida, we know that metaphysics is quite simply inescapable because we cannot find a language that is not already dominated by it and no-one knows this better than Heidegger (*Writing and Difference*, p. 280). The crucial thing to grasp about Derrida's readings of the history of philosophy, in other words, is that he is neither seeking to score points off metaphysics itself (as if anyone who believed in it were stupid or erroneous), nor to establish some new anti-metaphysical system (which would somehow avoid, or correct, the errors of its predecessor), so much as articulating this larger, and more complex, dilemma. There is an unavoidable sense in which every attempt to overcome metaphysics cannot help but repeat the language, discourse and assumptions of metaphysics, Derrida argues, because there is quite simply no other vocabulary available to us (*Positions*, p. 12). This is why Derrida admits right from the outset of his work that his own critique of metaphysics must necessarily work *within* the very system of ideas it wishes to contest even, at the risk of simply replicating it (*Grammatology*, p. 24/39).

In many ways, then, Derrida's greatest debt to Heidegger and the other anti-metaphysical philosophers we have mentioned is precisely this insight: any critique of metaphysics must reckon with *its own inherent tendency* to become metaphysical.

Martin Heidegger is one of the most famous philosophers of the twentieth century whose work is an indispensable touchstone for such movements as existentialism, deconstruction, hermeneutics and post-structuralist thought more generally. His philosophy takes the form of a new ontology, or science of being, that concerns itself with what it means 'to be'. On Heidegger's reading, it is crucial to distinguish between what he calls *Being* (*das Sein*), on the one hand, and particular *beings* or *entities* (*das Seiende*), on the other: 'The Being of entities "is" not itself an entity'.[10] To introduce the thesis of his seminal work *Being and Time*, Heidegger argues that the basic question 'What is Being?' has been largely forgotten by western philosophy because the latter focuses exclusively on beings or entities (*Being and Time*, p. 2). Heidegger seeks to recuperate the meaning of Being itself by focusing on a particular kind of being and the one he chooses is human being or, as he famously calls it, *Dasein* ('there-being'). For Heidegger, what defines *Dasein* is that it is not a being or entity that exists *in* time (like a rock or an animal) so much as a being who exists *as* time, whose being *is* essentially temporal: we are quite literally nothing other than the accumulation of our past experiences, on the one hand, and what we have the potential to 'project' out of those experiences into the future, on the other. If Heidegger is right to conclude that *Dasein* is an essentially *temporal* being, then this prepares the ground for his larger argument: the horizon for any understanding of the meaning of Being is *Time* (p. 1). The philosopher's later work broadens out to consider the history of philosophical interpretations of Being in the light of this relation between Being and Time. This body of work contends that the history of western metaphysics from Plato onwards is the story of the *reduction* of Being to a timeless, permanent 'present' being or entity that reaches its logical conclusion in the modern scientific concept of a graspable objective or empirical truth (p. 47). In his later writings, Heidegger undertakes what he calls a '*destruktion*' (meaning 'destruction', or more affirmatively, 'de-sedimentation' or even 'de-construction') of western metaphysics that seeks to reveal the originally historical, temporal encounter with Being that lies at the heart of every static, abstract or timeless concept of Being as presence (p. 44).

Between Phenomenology and Structuralism

Second, I would like to turn to a more immediate context for Derrida's thought. It will now be clear that *Of Grammatology* is immersed in the history of western philosophy, but in many ways the text is also the product of a set of contemporary debates within post-war French thought. As we'll see, Derrida negotiates his own philosophical position not simply via a reading of the history of metaphysics but through a close engagement with the two dominant intellectual currents within French thought of the 1960s: *phenomenology* and *structuralism*. To many contemporary eyes, phenomenology and structuralism represented two very different – indeed competing – attempts to get 'beyond' what were seen as the naïve prejudices or suppositions of traditional philosophy and to obtain a more rigorous account of reality. On the one hand, phenomenology tends to focus on the interior structure of our consciousness. On the other, structuralism seeks to offer a more objective analysis of the external structures of language, culture and society. More generally, phenomenologists and structuralists come to differing conclusions about what enables us to make sense of our experience of the world: Edmund Husserl argues that an *individual* act of consciousness 'intends' the objects it encounters, whereas Ferdinand de Saussure contends that objects only acquire meaning through their relative place within a more *general* linguistic or cultural system. If these two traditions in post-war thought appear to be in conflict with one another, though, Derrida's intriguing position is that both rely on the *same* logocentric or metaphysical tradition that we have seen at work in their philosophical predecessors. For Derrida, both traditions participate in the championing of speech as the true bearer of presence and the repression or marginalisation of writing as a base or empty vessel that is the logocentric gesture *par excellence*. In the remainder of this chapter, then, I want to offer a brief overview of Derrida's attempt to move beyond phenomenology and structuralism in the three major publications of 1967: *Speech and Phenomena*, *Writing and Difference* and, last not but least, *Of Grammatology*.

Phenomenology

First, we will look at Derrida's critique of the phenomenologist Edmund Husserl (1859–1938). As we have seen, Husserlian phenomenology provided Derrida with his own point of entry into philosophy: the young Derrida began a PhD thesis on Husserl and his first publication was a translation of an essay by the phenomenologist. However, it would be wrong to see Derrida as nothing more than a follower of Husserl because – for all his praise – his relation to his predecessor is increasingly critical. To put it in Derrida's own words, Husserlian phenomenology is the most 'modern, critical, and vigilant' form of the metaphysics of presence (*Positions*, p. 5). For Derrida, Husserl sets up *consciousness* as the site of a pure and immediate presence: our ego is present to itself in its own act of thinking without any intermediary and makes present the objects it intuits. In Derrida's account, however, Husserl's metaphysics of presence is in fact shot through with everything it wishes to exclude: absence, mediation, difference and, specifically, *writing*.

Edmund Husserl's phenomenology is complex and multi-faceted but we can define it very simply as an attempt to analyse the basic phenomena that present themselves to our conscious experience: the book you are holding in your hand, the desk at which you sit. It focuses on the *essence* of these particular 'intuitions', in other words, what your experience of them says about the way in which consciousness works more generally. According to Husserl, the defining characteristic of consciousness is that it is *intentional*, by which he means that it is always directed *towards* objects. To put it simply: consciousness is not an empty box into which objects are subsequently placed, but always the consciousness *of* some object. For Husserl, intentionality contains two, intrinsically linked, sides: the *noesis*, or intentional act of consciousness that is directed towards an object, and the object, or *noema*, towards which that act is directed. If this argument goes some way towards breaking down the subject/object dualism that has plagued philosophy since Descartes, it is important to bear in mind that Husserl's phenomenology remains at all times a theory of *consciousness*: what concerns him is purely that which presents itself to our conscious experience – a phenomenon – and he is careful not to make any presumptions about what may or may not lie behind that appearance. The intentional act can only be understood as what it is if we suspend or 'bracket' off – the key term Husserl uses here is *'epoché'* – all our everyday assumptions about the empirical existence of external objects (what he calls the 'natural attitude'), together with any prior philosophical assumptions or prejudices we might have about essence, existence or substance. This 'transcendental' attempt to clarify the pure or essential structures of consciousness by rigorously suspending or 'reducing' any presumption of the existence of the empirical world is increasingly criticised by Husserl's successors. In the view of later figures like Heidegger, Levinas and Ricoeur, Husserl's focus on the purity of consciousness risks becoming too abstract and theoretical in approach: phenomenology must take account of the *context* – linguistic, existential, ethical – in which consciousness is embedded.

1. To start with, I want to briefly outline Derrida's critique of Husserl in his first book *Speech and Phenomena*.[11] Derrida seeks to examine the relationship between consciousness and language in Husserl's famous *Logical Investigations*. It is here that Husserl's fragile belief in the 'presence' of consciousness – its supposed ability to operate without any intermediary such as language – can best be observed. First, Derrida notes how Husserl begins by drawing an important distinction between two different kinds of sign: an *expression* (*Ausdruck*) and an *indication* (*Anzeigen*).[12] On the one hand, expressions are 'meaningful signs' that directly express what the consciousness that uses them *wants or means* to say. On the other, indications are mere 'pointers' that lack an animating intention or meaning and infer or imply without delivering up an intention (*Logical Investigations*, pp. 269–70). Second, though, Derrida observes that Husserl goes on to associate expression with *speech* and indication with *writing*: speech is expressive because it necessarily entails the presence of the speaker, whereas writing is indicative because the writer is absent and substituted by a graphic inscription or mark. Unfortunately, though, things are not quite this simple because, as Derrida shows, the boundary between expression and indication, speech and writing and, more generally, presence and absence, constantly needs to be re-drawn. Straightaway, Husserl is forced to concede that not *all* speech is expressive: when we speak in order to communicate with someone else, our

words merely *indicate* our inner experience for the other person because, of course, they are not directly experiencing what we are experiencing. Now, this raises the inevitable question of *what* other, more expressive, form of speech there could be – for isn't speech *always* intended to communicate? – and Husserl's answer is what he calls the 'inner soliloquy of consciousness', that is, when we express ourselves to ourselves (*Logical Investigations*, pp. 278–9). Finally, then, Derrida shows how Husserl comes to the conclusion that it is only in our interior mental life that we achieve pure expression: our experiences are already present to us in our own consciousness, he argues, and so do not need to be 'communicated' in any way (*Speech and Phenomena*, p. 58). If Husserl thinks he has finally found a place where pure expression takes place – inside our own heads – Derrida shows that he is once again forced to concede that, even here, some *imaginary* form of communication remains: we talk, if only in an imaginary sense, to ourselves (*Logical Investigations*, p. 279). For Derrida, however, this is the point where the opposition between expression and indication – and everything that flows from it – finally breaks down: imagined communication is *still* communication, and, as Husserl himself argues, communication involves indication, and indication entails the *loss* of full presence. In this way, Derrida concludes that our consciousness cannot be 'present' to itself in the pure and immediate sense Husserl requires, because even its own *self-expression* is dependent upon language, mediation, *writing*: we communicate with *ourselves* in the same way that we would with another person.

2. According to Derrida, Husserl's phenomenology of time confirms this metaphysical commitment to 'presence' within his theory of consciousness. It is Husserl's contention that objects are *immediately* present to consciousness in both the spatial *and* the temporal senses of the word. When I 'intend' a certain object, it is present here and now to my consciousness: '[f]or the acts in question are themselves experienced by us at that very moment in the blink of an eye [*im selben Augenblick*]' (*Logical Investigations*, p. 280). Once again, however, Derrida uses an example from Husserl's *own* phenomenology – in this case his lectures on internal time consciousness – to show that the present moment in which perception takes place is in fact anything but 'present'. To clarify what might seem at face value to be a paradoxical argument, Derrida argues that what we perceive as the

'now' or present moment is in fact a *synthesis* or composite of memory and expectation, retention and protention. Derrida notes how Husserl himself shows us in *The Phenomenology of Internal Time Consciousness* that when we listen to a piece of music we retain the memory of the note just played, we hear the note currently being played, and anticipate the next note in the sequence, all at once. For Husserl, in other words, retention – the memory of what has *just* passed – is the 'tail' that always follows the 'comet' of primary impression.[13] If perception of the present is thus shot through with absence – what has just past and what is about to come – then Husserl's theory of consciousness is once again shown to be always and already conditioned by the kind of mediation that he brackets off as external or inessential to his phenomenology. Just as the *space* of consciousness is mediated by things that are not fully present – linguistic signs – so the *time* of consciousness is structured by what is temporally absent: the past and the future. In this sense, Husserl's metaphysics of 'presence' is once again forced to rely on the very thing it seeks to exclude: 'This alterity is in fact the very condition for presence' (*Speech and Phenomena*, p. 65).

3. Perhaps the closest Husserl comes to recognizing the role played by writing in his philosophy is in his intriguing late essay 'The Origin of Geometry'. As Derrida shows in his prize-winning introduction to that text (1962), it is here that the German philosopher does his utmost to square the circle between the transcendental and the material dimensions of his phenomenology by examining the role played by historical *tradition* in the formation of objective knowledge. Husserl begins his essay by asking the following question: what is it that enables a geometrical shape – and by extension, any ideal object that transcends time and space and exists absolutely identically for everyone – to appear in history for the first time?[14] First, and most obviously, Husserl says that the answer to this question is the *geometer* who invents such an object: Euclid, for instance, was the first person to recognise that any two points can be joined together by a straight line. Yet, what is it that makes geometrical principles stop being simply a subjective idea or impression in the mind of Euclid and start to become an objective truth that is recognised as such by everyone? For the later Husserl, the answer is language, and more precisely *writing*: it is only because Euclid wrote down his principles, in the form of the

Elements, that Euclidian geometry ceases to be just an idea in one man's head and becomes a universal objective truth (*Origin of Geometry*, pp. 163–4). Now, if it is actually the inscription of geometrical figures in repeatable graphic form that guarantees their ideal or objective status, then we have put our finger on another curious contradiction within Husserl's argument. On the one hand, geometry is *ideal*: it transcends time and space because it is the same everywhere and for everyone. On the other, geometry is paradoxically also *material*: its capacity to transcend time and space in this way actually depends upon it being *inscribed* in written form at a certain time and in a certain space. In this way, Derrida once again shows how Husserl's transcendental philosophy is in fact made possible, or conditioned, by the very thing it is supposed to transcend in the first place, namely, writing: 'Historical incarnation sets free the transcendental instead of binding it' (p. 77).

What, to summarise, does Derrida's – difficult and very technical – critique of Husserl add up to? To recall his premise, Derrida argues that Husserl's phenomenology remains – for all its undoubted commitment to philosophical rigour and objectivity – within a 'dogmatic or speculative' metaphysics of presence (*Speech and Phenomena*, pp. 4–5): Husserl simply *assumes* that truth is going to be equated with full presence, that presence is expressed in speech and that speech is superior to writing. It is also important to note the subtle way in which Derrida's own argument works here. As we have already begun to see, Derrida's critique of the limitations of metaphysics is not something that he *does to* it from the 'outside', so to speak, so much as something he demonstrates *about* it from within: Husserl's consistent attempts to privilege speech are constantly challenged, not by some new or better argument by Derrida himself, but by Husserl's own willingness, elsewhere in his work, to acknowledge the need for writing. If Husserl contradicts himself, however, Derrida makes clear that this is not because of some alleged 'naïvety' on his part (indeed he has nothing but praise for the rigour and ingenuity of Husserl's arguments) but rather because it is symptomatic of a *larger* and insoluble problem which goes to the heart of metaphysics itself (pp. 4–5). For Derrida, in other words, Husserl's phenomenology shows us that, *even in its most rigorous philosophical form*, the metaphysics of presence depends upon a foundational instability: the promotion of truth, presence and speech is always bought at the expense of a repression of mediation, language and *writing*. In this way, Derrida's critique of metaphysics takes him beyond what is traditionally understood as the domain of 'philosophy' and into the field of what, in France, are called the human sciences: linguistics, literature, psychoanalysis and the then-dominant intellectual movement called 'structuralism'.

Structuralism
Second, then, I want to turn to Derrida's critique of structuralism. As we have hinted, structuralism provides the second indispensable point of reference for Derrida's early work: many of his early writings consist of readings of key figures within this movement such as, for example, Ferdinand de Saussure and Claude Lévi-Strauss. However, once again Derrida is by no means a passive adherent to structuralism, but a major critic of its guiding premises and suppositions. To put it in a nutshell, Derrida's argument is that structuralism – for all the force of its critique of so-called 'transcendental' philosophy – is still guided by an entirely metaphysical belief in 'presence'. For Derrida, in other words, structuralism is not structuralist all the way down: it presumes a fixed or 'present' point around which every structure revolves. In Derrida's account, however, this desire for a full presence at the heart of every structure is, once again, only possible on the basis of the repression of mediation, difference and *writing*.

Ferdinand de Saussure (1857–1913) was a linguist but is now commonly held to be the 'father' of the modern movement called structuralism. He focused his research less on particular units of language – what he calls '*parole*' or speech – so much as on the underlying *system* of language (*langue*) in which those units exist. He famously argues that individual units of language acquire meaning from their relative position within the linguistic system as a whole: a word like 'cat', for example, has no meaning outside the system of the English language.[15] It is this shift from the specific to the general that opens structuralism and Saussure's insights were taken up, worked over and generalised by a range of thinkers working in the humanities and the social sciences in the post-war period including, most famously, the anthropologist Claude Lévi-Strauss who applied structuralist principles to the analysis of a South American tribespeople called the Nambikwara. At the time Derrida was writing the *Grammatology*, structuralism had been transformed into nothing less than a full-blown 'science of man' that sought to show how human experience can only be understood by relating it to pre-existing linguistic, cultural and social systems. To be clear, then, structuralism travels in the exact *opposite* direction to Husserl's transcendental phenomenology: whereas phenomenology, in at least some of its forms, tries to bracket off culture in order to focus purely on what presents itself to our conscious experience, structuralism insists that such experience is *only* possible on the basis of the linguistic or cultural systems of meaning that phenomenology seeks to exclude. For Saussure and his followers, in other words, consciousness is always mediated through a prior network of signs, concepts, and values which enable us to make sense of our experience and, in this respect, at least, it would seem to confirm Derrida's own critique of phenomenology. More generally, as we will see in Part 2, structuralism institutes a differential and relational theory of meaning that will be an enormous influence upon Derridaean deconstruction. Just as a single chess piece only makes sense in the context of the other pieces on the board, so no individual unit within a network has meaning in itself but rather achieves meaning in relation to all the other units within the system. If structuralism undoubtedly represented a powerful critique of the supposed purity of transcendental phenomenology, however, a new generation of philosophers increasingly accused structuralists of trading one kind of purism for another: Saussure and his followers are convicted of advancing an excessively abstract or theoretical concept of language, culture and history as if these could be reduced to a sort of computer programme. In the view of avowedly *post*-structuralist critics such as Jacques Lacan, Michel Foucault and the later Roland Barthes, structuralism offers – for all its undoubted insights – a somewhat fixed, static and determinist account of the way in which linguistic and cultural systems work.

1. To start with, it is helpful to look at Derrida's critique of the work of the structuralist anthropologist Claude Lévi-Strauss (1908–) in a famous essay called 'Structure, Sign and Play in the Discourse of the Human Sciences' that was first published in the collection *Writing and Difference* (1967). Derrida begins this essay by effectively seeking to turn the tables on structuralism itself: what, he asks, *structures* the search for structures of language, culture and society? As we have already begun to see, his answer to this question is that structuralism is characterised by the attempt to identify a fixed point or centre at the heart of every structure (*Writing and Difference*, p. 278). Now, this idea of a 'centre' has a complex relation to the structure which surrounds it. On the one hand, a centre must be *within* any given structure: it gives form, order or balance to that structure, just as, say, a pivot or fulcrum enables something to move around it. On the other, however, a centre is also paradoxically *outside* a given structure: it is the very thing that governs or controls that structure, in the same way that a pivot or fulcrum controls movement, while itself remaining motionless. For Derrida, then, it becomes clear that structuralism is curiously self-exempting: *everything* has a structure – a relative place within the play of the system – *except* the centre of the structure itself where that play comes to a stop (p. 279). In this sense, we can begin to see the structuralist project as another manifestation of the metaphysics of presence that seeks to locate a pure or original essence or foundation that underlies all mediation: it conceives of structure 'on the basis of a full presence which is beyond play' (p. 279). What form, though, does this desire for 'full presence' take within Lévi-Strauss's structuralist anthropology?

2. As we will see in more detail later on, Derrida identifies a number of ways in which Lévi-Strauss's field work among the Nambikwara tribespeople remains trapped within a metaphysics of presence. First, Derrida argues that Lévi-Strauss's self-styled 'scientific' methodology is recognisably part of a philosophical heritage that stretches at least as far back as the eighteenth-century philosopher Jean-Jacques Rousseau. Of course, Lévi-Strauss is well aware of the dubious nature of such abstract and simplistic philosophical categories as the nature/culture opposition but he continues to use them as explanatory tools even when faced by cases – such as the incest taboo – that cannot be accommodated within them. He justifies this strategy as a form of '*bricolage*' – a 'do it yourself' process of assemblage – which entitles him

to borrow whatever idea is at hand if it proves useful, without having to accept it as objectively true.[16] Unfortunately, this *ad hoc* approach sits rather uneasily with his ambition to construct a rigorous science of culture (pp. 283–6). Second, Derrida argues that Lévi-Strauss also relies on a metaphysical concept of history. If Lévi-Strauss is rightly suspicious of a Eurocentric model of history as a progression from savagery to modern civilisation, the anthropologist's attempt to bracket off that history and analyse the structure of primitive societies purely on their own terms risks establishing a static or timeless idea of culture. For Derrida, as we will see in more detail later on, what this means is that Lévi-Strauss is unable to account for the *genesis* of structures – how primitive cultures came into being, changed over time, and gave way to others – except in terms of a catastrophic 'fall' from the primitive to the civilised (p. 292). Finally, and, for our purposes, most importantly, Derrida speculates that structuralist anthropology is motivated by a thoroughly *logocentric* 'nostalgia for origins': Lévi-Strauss argues that the Nambikwara tribespeople exist in a state of 'natural innocence' and this purity is epitomised by the fact that they only communicate via *speech* (p. 292). The difference between primitive and civilised societies – between the world of the Nambikwara Indians and modern Europe – is thus represented as an opposition between oral and written culture. This opposition between speech and writing is, in turn, transformed into an ethical *hierarchy* between the innocence enjoyed by the tribespeople and the violence and corruption of European colonialism. In the *Grammatology*, however, Derrida will question whether this state of pure presence beyond all mediation ever actually exists.

3. We are now in a position to grasp *why* Derrida thinks that Lévi-Strauss – and the structuralist project more generally – remains so firmly within a metaphysics of presence. It seems odd, on the face of it, to accuse structuralism of being metaphysical given that it tries so hard to move *beyond* what it saw as the abstractions of traditional philosophy in order to obtain a more concrete and systematic account of reality in terms of, say, language. However, we already know that Derrida is deeply suspicious of any attempt to step 'outside' the illusions of metaphysics for the very simple reason that we have no way of thinking, not even the language of transgression or overcoming, that does not stem from metaphysics itself. As he constantly makes

clear, structuralism – like phenomenology before it – remains caught within the vicious circle that plagues any anti-metaphysical movement: every critique of metaphysics cannot avoid using the language of metaphysics. Quite simply, structuralism's attempt to just *stop doing* philosophy and begin again with something more 'scientific' and 'objective' like anthropology, linguistics or history leaves its own deepest metaphysical assumptions unquestioned. If structuralism continually throws up new scientific methodologies – Saussure's linguistics, Lévi-Strauss's ethnography, Michel Foucault's archaeology or Pierre Bourdieu's sociology – in order to get around old metaphysical problems, Derrida argues that all these supposedly original approaches actually presuppose some of the most ancient philosophical oppositions imaginable: speech and writing, nature and culture, the transcendental and the empirical, and so on. For Derrida, this double-bind often results in some cruel ironies: Lévi-Strauss's structuralist anthropology is an entirely commendable attempt to get beyond Eurocentric presuppositions and consider different cultures on their own terms but, as we have already begun to see, his anthropology is entirely the product of a European philosophical tradition (p. 282). In other words, Lévi-Strauss starts out trying to *repair* the offence caused by cultural imperialism – where European values are imposed on other peoples as if they were universal standards – but he merely ends up *compounding* it because his ethnological project is complicit with what Derrida calls the 'most original and powerful ethnocentrism' of all: *logocentrism*.

What, then, should we take away from Derrida's critique of structuralism? To recap, Derrida's hypothesis is that – for all his scientific credentials – Lévi-Strauss's structuralist anthropology remains 'caught . . . within the metaphysics – logocentrism – which at the same time [he] claims rather precipitately to have "gone beyond"' (*Grammatology*, p. 99/148): Lévi-Strauss, like Husserl before him, takes a more or less arbitrary *decision* that truth will equal presence which, in turn, will be equated with speech. Once again, it is interesting to observe the working method that leads Derrida to this controversial conclusion. Just as we saw in his engagement with phenomenology, Derrida demonstrates structuralism's limitations and inconsistencies from the *inside* instead of subjecting it to an external critique: Lévi-Strauss the scientist is confronted by Lévi-Strauss the pragmatic *bricoleur*, just as Husserl was contested on strict Husserlian grounds. If Lévi-Strauss is accorded a privileged place in Derrida's work (p. 99/148), it is not to castigate him for some individual error or naïveté on his part (once again Derrida lavishes praise upon his ingenious attempts to get around intractable problems), but because he is a symptom of what we have seen to be the larger instability of the metaphysical edifice itself. For Derrida, in other words, what Lévi-Strauss's structuralism teaches us is that *even the most rigorous disciplines outside the province of philosophy* remain caught within the foundational incoherence of the metaphysics of presence because, once again, their sponsorship of truth, presence and speech is bought and paid for by the repression of mediation, difference, writing. In this way, Derrida's critique of metaphysics inevitably takes us *beyond* the domain of structuralism as well as phenomenology.

Between Phenomenology and Structuralism

What, then, is at stake in Derrida's intricate negotiation with phenomenology and structuralism? It is clear that Derrida sees the rivalry between the two dominant schools of post-war French thought as a contemporary manifestation of the either/or logic that dominates the metaphysics of presence. As we have already suggested, phenomenology and structuralism seem to represent two very different ways of obtaining a more rigorous account of reality than that which seems to be afforded by traditional philosophical categories. Either we examine phenomena just as they appear to us and bracket off all speculations about the world outside our consciousness or we suspend the subjective bias of consciousness itself and offer a rigorous and systematic analysis of social structures. However, what start out as two diametrically opposed theories – the one philosophical, the other drawn from the social sciences, the one transcendental, the other empirical or positivist – strangely end up meeting in the middle. To put it bluntly, Derrida argues that phenomenology and structuralism *turn into* one another:

1. First, Derrida shows that each discipline relies on a thoroughly metaphysical idea of full and unmediated *presence* as the ground of its theory: phenomenology is based upon the pure *interiority* of consciousness, whereas structuralism is predicated upon the pure formality of linguistic or cultural *systems*. In this sense, both disciplines

agree that it is possible to locate a pure presence even if they disagree about where this presence can be found.

2. We have also seen that both phenomenology and structuralism are what Derrida calls *logocentric* discourses. In both cases, the *voice* is identified as the privileged medium by which 'presence' is communicated: Husserl's phenomenology argues that speech is closer to the pure self-expression of consciousness than writing, whereas Lévi-Strauss's structuralist anthropology champions the innocence and authenticity of oral culture over its written counterpart.

3. Perhaps more importantly, both phenomenology and structuralism share what we are beginning to see is the fate of any metaphysics of presence. Any attempt to establish a value as 'present' – whether it be the soul or the body, the transcendental or the empirical, consciousness or language – implicitly depends on the value it marks as 'absent'. Each theory claims to offer exclusive access to knowledge but phenomenology and structuralism are locked in a mutually dependent relationship whereby the one always requires the other in order to make good its own pretensions. On the one hand, phenomenology's attempt to offer a transcendental theory of knowledge always seems to run up against the kind of empirical territory – the essential role played by writing, language, culture in the constitution of consciousness – that is the province of structuralism. On the other, structuralism's attempt to offer a more empirical or scientific theory of knowledge than that afforded by philosophy always remains caught within the very philosophical assumptions – the inescapability of such ideas as truth, presence, universality when we want to talk about language – that it is seeking to move beyond.

Finally, then, we can begin to see that Derrida's critique of the two dominant traditions within post-war French thought affords him a point of access to the much bigger task of articulating what he takes to be the originary state of mediation, relation or difference that lies beneath every metaphysics of presence: we cannot ultimately separate phenomenology and structuralism from one another. If we cannot simply *choose* between the two, it is necessary to construct a philosophy that explores this point where phenomenology and structuralism meet but which, strictly speaking, belongs to neither. What, then, is the best way of talking about this position that lies *between* phenomenology and structuralism and, more generally, between transcendental and empirical theories of knowledge? Can we come up with a way of articulating it that does not fall into the rival traps of *either* accepting the old philosophical categories uncritically *or* acting as if we can somehow leave them behind altogether and invent some brand new way of thinking? To what extent, in other words, might it be possible to move beyond the false opposition of simply *accepting* metaphysics (as if there were nothing wrong with it) and *rejecting* it (as if there were something better we could use instead) by seeking to demonstrate the contingency of that system of thought from *within* its own perimeters? In *Of Grammatology*, as we will see, the name of this critical procedure is 'deconstruction'.

Conclusion

In concluding this brief sketch of the historical context of the *Grammatology*, I want to say a word about Derrida's own philosophy of history. It will hopefully be clear by now that his philosophy does not simply fall out of the sky. On the contrary, it emerges from a profound, if always critical, engagement with both the contemporary debates of post-war French thought (phenomenology versus structuralism) and the much longer history of anti-metaphysical philosophy (Nietzsche, Freud and Heidegger). Quite simply, Derrida's philosophy could be said to ask a question that is as almost as old as philosophy itself: to what extent is it possible to establish a more secure basis of knowledge than that offered by metaphysics? If Derrida's work has a history, though, it also forces us to consider exactly what we *mean* by the term 'history' and its various correlates: context, tradition, lineage, heritage and so on. For Derrida, as we suggested at the beginning of this chapter, the traditional philosophical concept of 'history' is itself the product of the metaphysical assumptions he is attempting to call into question and this claim has important implications for any attempt to write a history of his thought.

To be sure, Derrida regards himself as a deeply historical thinker: 'I consider myself very much a historian', he once said, adding that *Of Grammatology* 'is a history book through and through'.[17] It is not enough to say that Derrida offers a new history of philosophy, however, because his work also offers a radically new philosophy of history. First,

Derrida's critique of metaphysics is in many ways an attempt to reveal what we might call the radical *historicity* of the present. As he consistently argues, what appear to be timeless or natural ideas – 'being', 'truth' etc. – are actually anything but. Yet, this argument also applies to the philosophical idea of 'history' itself, our very understanding of what history is and how it works. Second, then, Derrida's work also reveals that the philosophy of history – which stretches from Aristotle, through Hegel, up to Heidegger – is itself the product of a metaphysics of presence. For Derrida, as he makes clear on a number of occasions, the philosophical idea of history relies on a tripartite assumption of *linearity* (the idea of time as a continuous line of present moments), of *teleology* (where history is seen as the progression towards an ultimate goal or endpoint), and of *tradition* (where history is understood as the gradual stockpiling or accumulation of knowledge) which is entirely metaphysical in origin (*Positions*, p. 57). If what we understand as 'history' depends upon a metaphysics of presence, Derrida's aim is once again to show how that idea of history is *itself* a historical construction: it cannot be taken as truth. Finally, then, Derrida's critique of the philosophical concept of 'history' seeks to do what he does to any other metaphysical idea, namely, to reveal the open-ended network of differences on which it resides: no historical moment, body of thought, epoch or tradition, is ever wholly at one with itself because it inevitably contains the traces of what precedes and follows it. In Derrida's hands, what we might call the metaphysical concept of history – where a succession of present moments are strung together like pearls on a necklace – begins to unravel into a more complex, plural or differential set of relations between past, present and future: 'there is not one single history, a general history, but rather histories' (p. 58).

What, then, are the implications of Derrida's philosophy of history for our own attempt to offer a history of his thought? It will hopefully be obvious that Derrida would want to question many of the underlying assumptions about the way in which history works that have informed this chapter: this is another way in which his work challenges the very idea of a 'philosophical guide book'. As a consequence, we must resist any attempt to see 'Derrida' as simply one more chapter in the long history of ideas because it is precisely this idea of history – as linear, progressive, cumulative, and, above all, 'present' – that he most wishes to contest. To put it simply, Derrida's work always has *more* than one history and it would be possible to re-write our own history of his thought in many different ways. First of all, it would be just as easy to find the roots of deconstruction in Plato and Aristotle as it is to discover them in Husserl and Heidegger, for example, not to mention in a range of figures and texts from outside philosophy such as Shakespeare, Joyce, Blanchot, Kafka or Celan: 'everything is in Shakespeare' Derrida himself admits (*Acts of Literature*, p. 67). Yet why stop there? If his philosophy is concerned with identifying nothing less than the hidden condition of all thought whatsoever – what lies beneath the western tradition in its entirety – there is no reason why we should not find the traces of Derrida every-where, even or especially in fields, disciplines or modes of thought that he, personally, does not, or cannot, enter: theology, for example. Perhaps the single biggest problem with any attempt to offer a 'history' of Derrida's philosophy, however, is that such a process almost inevitably assumes that this thought is somehow past, com-plete or done with. For Derrida himself, the great texts of the history of philosophy were not dusty relics but inexhaustible resources and the task of reading them will never be finished: 'I always have the feeling that, despite centuries of reading, these texts remain untouched, withdrawn into a reserve, still to come'.[18] If this is true for Plato and Aristotle, then it might be equally true for *Of Grammatology*: its significance does not lie behind us, in an era that is now disap-pearing into history, but rather in front of us, as something still to be decided upon, debated, *read*. In this sense, we might argue that the most important historical context for Derrida's work is the *future*.

Notes

1. This chapter is by necessity very selective. It focuses on only a few of Derrida's precursors and ignores some major interlocutors such as Plato, Aristotle, Kant and Hegel, not to mention contemporaries like Levinas and Blanchot. As will become clear, my aim is only to offer a – brief – exposition of Derrida's readings of figures like Husserl and Lévi-Strauss: I cannot enter into the vast and complex question of whether those readings are accurate in every respect. In the notes, I provide ref-erences for primary texts which will allow interested readers to decide such questions for themselves.

2. René Descartes, *Meditations on First Philosophy* trans. John Cottingham (Cambridge: Cambridge University Press, 1986), pp. 16–23.

3. Karl Marx and Friedrich Engels, *The German Ideology* (London: Lawrence & Wishart, 1970), p. 47. All further references will be abbreviated in the text.

4. Karl Marx, 'Contribution to the Critique of Hegel's Philosophy of Right', in *On Religion* (Atlanta: Scholars Press, 1993), pp. 41–2.

5. Jacques Derrida, *Specters of Marx: The State of the Debt, the Work of Mourning and the New International*, trans. Peggy Kamuf (New York and London: Routledge, 1994). All further references will be abbreviated in the text.

6. Friedrich Nietzsche, *On the Genealogy of Morality*, trans. Maudemarie Clark and Alan J. Swensen (Indianapolis, IN and Cambridge: Hackett, 1998), §24, p. 110.

7. Jacques Derrida, *Margins of Philosophy*, trans. Alan Bass (New York: Harvester, 1982), pp. 17–18, 109–37, 207–72, 273–306. All further references will be abbreviated in the text.

8. Sigmund Freud, 'Beyond the Pleasure Principle' (1920), in *On Metapsychology: The Theory of Psychoanalysis*, ed. Angela Richards, trans. James Strachey, Penguin Freud Library, vol. 11 (Harmondsworth: Penguin, 1991), p. 295.

9. To begin with, however, it is interesting to note that Derrida still used the term 'destruction' as opposed to 'deconstruction' in the original version of the *Grammatology*. This was published in the form of two lengthy review articles in the journal *Critique* (December 1965–January 1966).

10. Martin Heidegger, *Being and Time*, trans. John Macquarrie and Edward Robinson (Oxford: Blackwell, 1962), p. 26. All further references will be abbreviated in the text.

11. Jacques Derrida, *Speech and Phenomena and Other Essays on Husserl's Theory of Signs*, ed. and trans. David Allison (Evanston, IL: Northwestern University Press, 1973). All further references will be abbreviated in the text.

12. Edmund Husserl, *Logical Investigations*, trans. J. N. Findlay (New York: Humanities Press, 1970). All further references will be abbreviated in the text.

13. Edmund Husserl, *The Phenomenology of Internal Time Consciousness*, trans. James Churchill (Bloomington, IN: Indiana University Press, 1964), pp. 50–1. For Derrida, Husserl does not fully capitalise on his own

insight: the phenomenologist stresses the originary 'present' impression at the expense of the retention and protentions that also comprise the process of perception.

14. Jacques Derrida, *Edmund Husserl's* Origin of Geometry: *An Introduction*, trans. John P. Leavey (Lincoln, NE and London: University of Nebraska Press, 1989). All further references will be abbreviated in the text.

15. Ferdinand de Saussure, *Course in General Linguistics*, trans. Wade Baskin (New York: McGraw-Hill, 1959, 2nd edn 1966). All further references will be abbreviated in the text.

16. Claude Lévi-Strauss, *The Savage Mind*, trans. John Weightman and Doreen Weightman (London: George Weidenfeld and Nicolson, 1967), p. 17.

17. Jacques Derrida, *Acts of Literature*, ed. Derek Attridge (London and New York: Routledge, 1992), p. 67. All further references will be abbreviated in the text.

18. Jacques Derrida, *Points . . . Interviews 1974–1994*, ed. Elisabeth Weber, trans. Peggy Kamuf *et al.* (Stanford, CA: Stanford University Press, 1995), p. 82.

2. A Guide to the Text

The Beginning of Writing

In the opening chapter of the *Grammatology*, Derrida begins to map out what he calls a 'theoretical matrix' for the book as a whole (p. lxxxix/7). His purpose is both to identify certain privileged historical moments or figures for study – Ferdinand de Saussure, Claude Lévi-Strauss and Jean-Jacques Rousseau – and to establish a new critical vocabulary – deconstruction, writing, the trace – with which to discuss them. As we have already seen in our introduction, the *Grammatology* is an extremely ambitious book that attempts nothing less than a wholesale re-reading of the western tradition. To recap what we have learnt so far, Derrida is going to argue that the western philosophical tradition is a *metaphysics of presence* in the sense that it consistently and dogmatically posits a moment of pure and unmediated 'presence' – something that is simply or really 'there' – as the supreme or universal value. Second, he will contend that the defining mode of that metaphysics of presence is *logocentrism*: speech is deemed to be the privileged vehicle of this presence whereas writing is said to represent the mediation or deferment of that presence. Finally, and most importantly, Derrida will propose that the metaphysical or logocentric commitment to speech depends upon a foundational contradiction or tension: all language – both speech and writing – is characterised by the essential *mediation* that metaphysics historically assigns to 'writing' alone. If the guarantee of truth – speech – is already contaminated with 'writing', we will also begin to see that this has important implications for our concept of a pure and unmediated 'presence' itself: we cannot gain access to a presence – a 'there' – that exists wholly independently of linguistic mediation. For Derrida, as we will now see, the theory of the *linguistic sign* represents a privileged symptom of this entire problematic: it is the sign – more than anything else – that is the site of his questioning of logocentrism. What, then, is Derrida's argument?

Deconstruction

First, however, I want to briefly discuss a famous term that appears in this opening chapter: *deconstruction*. To introduce his own reading of logocentrism, Derrida somewhat mysteriously says that what is required is 'not the demolition, but the de-sedimentation, the *deconstruction*' of the *logos*' (p. 10/21). What exactly does this mean? It is important to note straightaway that Derrida only uses the term 'deconstruction' very sparingly in his early work and in very specific contexts: what is surprising for new readers is how little it appears in the *Grammatology*, not how much. Nowhere does he suggest that it is the 'proper name' for his own way of doing philosophy. Yet, as his reputation grew, any precise or technical meaning that 'deconstruction' once possessed was quickly lost, and the term has become synonymous with Derrida's thought in general: we now speak of 'Derridaean deconstruction' in the same way we would of 'Humean empiricism' or 'Kantian transcendental idealism'. If the specific term 'deconstruction' has been misapplied, however, it has also been widely misunderstood: Derrida's philosophy has, we have seen, been celebrated or attacked as everything from a liberal or anarchic philosophy of freedom, choice and difference to a form of extreme scepticism, relativism or even nihilism. Let's see what Derrida himself says.

To start with, Derrida always stresses that 'deconstruction' is *not* to be confused with a simple process of philosophical destruction or demolition: he is not interested in simply taking things apart. As its unusual etymology – with those two apparently contradictory prefixes 'de-' and 'con-' rubbing shoulders against one another – suggests, 'deconstruction' actually describes a double process that is *both* positive *and* negative, both destructive *and* constructive. On the one hand, it undoubtedly performs a negative or critical role in undoing, dismantling or questioning the way in which any given system is put together. On the other, however, it has a deeply positive dimension because – in a way that is at least partially analogous to Heidegger's '*destruktion*' of

the history of ontology – its purpose is not to destroy but to re-con-
struct, re-constitute or re-affirm any structure. If deconstruction is
actually an exercise in 'reconstruction', however, it does not seek to put
things back together exactly as they were. For Derrida, what deconstruction attempts to do is to articulate the – often hidden or
repressed – conditions according to which it is possible for any structure to be constituted in the first place. In Derrida's own words, deconstruction signifies the 'undoing, decomposing and de-sedimenting of
structures' *in order to* 'understand how an "ensemble" was constituted
and to reconstruct it to this end'.[1]

Who – if anyone – *performs* this 'deconstruction'? It is also important to stress that 'deconstruction' is not a new theory, technique or
methodology that we can simply apply to particular texts in the way
that we might, for example, do a Marxist or a Freudian 'reading' of
a novel. As we have already begun to see by looking at the way in
which Derrida reads Husserl and Lévi-Strauss, deconstruction is not
something we *do* to a text from the 'outside', so to speak, so much as
something that we *reveal about* the way in which any text is internally
constructed. If Derrida's reading of the privileged texts of logocentrism has a purpose, it is not to establish some superior position of
knowledge or authority so much as to tease out the immanent contradictions within the texts themselves: Husserl is criticised by none
other than Husserl and Lévi-Strauss by no one but Lévi-Strauss.
Quite simply, 'deconstruction' is less the name of a *tool* or instrument
that we apply to a text than of a basic – if hidden or repressed – *condition* of every text. Every text is based upon a shifting network of
mediations, differences and traces. For Derrida, then, the process of
reading is not a question of actively 'deconstructing' logocentrism so
much as showing that the metaphysics of presence is *already* in a
process of what we might call 'self-deconstruction' insofar as it has a
'self' at all: it has no full or 'present' ground or foundation on which
to base itself and so it exists in a permanent state of instability or contingency. In Geoffrey Bennington's succinct phrase, then, we might
say that Derrida does not so much 'deconstruct metaphysics' – in the
way that we might dismantle a car engine – as reveal something called
'*metaphysics in deconstruction*': what we call 'deconstruction' is a name for
a structural or foundational instability on which, despite appearances
to the contrary, every metaphysical system is erected.[2]

'*ce qui arrive*'

The Epoch of the Book

I now want to move on to Derrida's – very brief – account of the history of western metaphysics at the start of the chapter 'The End of the Book and the Beginning of Writing'. It is only possible to understand what is so new about 'grammatology' – the science of which now shows signs of 'liberation' all over the world (p. 4/13) – by seeing it against the historical backdrop of logocentrism. As we have already suggested, Derrida decides to focus his analysis on *one* particular aspect of this history: the linguistic sign. Yet, how can he justify this decision to look at just one single – even marginal – aspect of logocentrism at the expense of all others? For Derrida, the simple answer to this question is that the linguistic sign is never simply one example of logocentrism among others, but rather a *defining point of entry* into the logic of metaphysics as a whole. The logocentric theory of the sign is, as we will see, predicated upon an opposition between what are today called the 'signifier' and the 'signified'. This opposition leads us, in turn, into the larger network of oppositions that comprise metaphysics in its entirety: soul/body, infinite/finite, transcendental/empirical. In this sense, Derrida's deconstruction of the theory of the sign is the thread that enables him to unravel the system of logocentrism as a whole.

Aristotle

First, Derrida's history goes back to the very beginnings of western metaphysics itself. Aristotle's *De Interpretatione* (*On Interpretation*) is one of the foundational texts for the logocentric theory of the linguistic sign. It establishes an absolutely fundamental point about the sign that will endure all the way up to the present day: a sign is always a sign or re-presentation *of* some pre-existing idea or mental experience.[3] Accordingly, Aristotle institutes a distinction at the heart of the sign between what modern linguists call the 'signifier' and the 'signified': a given sound or mark (a signifier) relates to a given idea or concept (a signified). However, Aristotle then goes on to draw an – equally crucial – distinction between two different *kinds* of signs or signifiers: the spoken and the written. On the one hand, he argues that speech has a relationship of immediate proximity with our mental experiences because it expresses what we are thinking without any mediation or substitute whatsoever. On the other, he argues that writing has, at best, an indirect or mediated relation to our mental experiences because it substitutes a set of material inscriptions – a mark on a piece of paper for example – for thought. If speech directly signifies the ideas or intentions of the person speaking, in other words, writing only has a second-hand relation to thought because it is nothing more than *a sign of a sign*. The written signifier is merely the sign of the spoken signifier, in other words, whereas the spoken signifier is the sign of the signified idea or thought. This means that there is a clear logical and indeed chronological hierarchy between the spoken and the written word as modes of signification. For Aristotle, speech is deemed to be chronologically prior to writing: the written word is *phonetic* in origin, that is to say, it is derived from, and imitates, the original act of language that is speech. In Derrida's account, however, this whole theory of the sign is – for all its undoubted power – deeply complicit with the metaphysics of presence he wishes to call into question: we will see in the next section that the sign can never be truly described as simply the sign *of* some pre-existing immediate, self-present idea or signified.

Christian Theology

According to Derrida, another key moment in the history of the sign is what he calls the 'epoch of Christian creationism or infinitism' where Christian theology and Greek metaphysics meet (p. 13/24). It is, he argues, via the theological distinction between the sensible and the intelligible world – 'this' world and the 'other' world – that the modern linguistic distinction between the signifier and the signified comes into being: the 'face of the sign', he memorably writes, is turned towards the 'face of God' (p. 13/24). Quite simply, Derrida's contention is that the spoken or written sign is always the sign of a realm that exists prior to, and *independently* of, the sensible world whether it be the mind of god or, as we will see later on in the case of Ferdinand de Saussure, merely an intelligible idea or concept. Either way, he argues, it contains a 'metaphysico-theological' dimension (p. 13/25). Yet, Derrida goes on to identify a more profound way in which the concept of the sign remains theological, even in its apparently most modern and scientific forms. For Derrida, the sign is always taken to be the sign of a pure or immediate *presence* that lies behind it and this metaphysics of presence finds its most systematic expression in Christianity: what characterises the God of medieval scholastic theology, he argues, is that it is a first cause (*Causa sui*), an unmoved mover, in short, an absolutely present being who guarantees all meaning (p. 71/104). If Saussure and other modern linguists obviously dispense with any belief in a creator god lying behind the sign, Derrida has little difficulty in showing that they still retain a residually theological investment in what he calls a 'transcendental signified' – an ultimate presence – which anchors all meaning in itself: the presence of God is merely replaced by the presence of the speaker, of his or her thoughts and feelings, and so on. In this sense, Derrida argues that the age of the sign is essentially *theological*: 'the sign and divinity have the same place and time of birth' (p. 14/25).

From Rousseau to Heidegger

For Derrida, we can trace the evolution of logocentrism from Greek metaphysics, through Christian theology all the way up to the present day and even beyond: 'Perhaps it will never *end*' (p. 14/25). It is simply a matter of trading in one idea of the *logos* for another as we move through history: Christian theology's God, Descartes's thinking or knowing subject, Nietzsche's will to power and so on. After Descartes, for instance, logocentrism takes on a new form: the spoken word no longer refers to the presence of god but to the self-presence of the thinking or feeling subject. Who are the key exemplars of modern logocentrism? To begin with, Derrida argues that a privileged place in this new epoch must be accorded to the eighteenth-century Enlightenment philosopher Jean-Jacques Rousseau: we are, as we will see later on in this book, apparently still living in the 'age' of Rousseau. However, things don't stop there. Derrida suggests that Hegel's speculative philosophy represents another key moment in the history of logocentrism. Hegel famously argues that we can see the history of philosophy as a gradual progression through a series of dialectical resolutions towards a position of absolute knowledge or spirit (*Geist*). Unfortunately, the German philosopher still privileges *phonetic* writing – writing which imitates speech – as the medium by which knowledge has been preserved and transmitted throughout history because, once again, he believes speech to be closest to pure thought. Finally, and as we have already seen in the previous section, Derrida contends that even the self-professedly 'anti-metaphysical' philosophers of the last hundred years – Nietzsche and Heidegger – do not entirely escape from the logocentric enclosure. We might like to think that Nietzsche's theory of 'perspectivism' – which insists on the endless process of interpretation and the impossibility of arriving at a single truth – manages to turn logocentrism upside down but, as Heidegger argues in a famous critique,[4] this gesture of *reversal* still remains controlled by the either/or logic it is seeking to overthrow (p. 19/31-2). If he at least partially subscribes to Heidegger's view of Nietzsche's philosophy as a kind of 'inverted Platonism', however, Derrida remains deeply sceptical about Heidegger's own attempt to escape the illusions of metaphysics. In the final section of this chapter, he devotes several complex pages (pp. 19-24/31-8) to arguing that – for all his claims about the endless withdrawal of Being – Heidegger's attempt to articulate an 'originary truth' beyond the metaphysics of presence serves to 'reinstate' the old theological idea of a 'transcendental signified' which guarantees all meaning.

The End of the Book?

We still need to be clear about what Derrida is – and is not – arguing about the history of logocentrism here. It is not that this history is simply 'wrong' or that we can leave it behind us and progress to something better. On the contrary, it is indispensable: we would not be able to think without it because it is quite simply the history of philosophy itself (p. 14/25). To go back to where we started, Derrida's aim is to show logocentrism in *deconstruction*: he *both* questions its self-construction – the 'official' story it tells itself about the way in which it is organised – *and* shows how it can be re-constructed otherwise. As we have seen, it will always be possible to write the history of logocentrism differently because it is founded on an instability that means it can never make good on its own claims to authenticity: no text, author or tradition is thus ever purely or simply logocentric. To accept the logocentric story of the sign at face value, we have seen, is to equate speech with pure presence and writing with mediation, difference or even absence. However, we will see later on that *all* signs are characterised by this state of mediation – which makes it impossible for them to directly relate to a 'present' meaning or signified – and so what logocentrism attributes to 'writing' actually describes the state of language as such. Now, this state of affairs casts an entirely new light on the history of logocentrism we have just been narrating, Derrida argues. For Derrida, writing actually occupies a contradictory position within the history of logocentrism if we look more closely at the way in which that history is constructed: the written word will not stay in the lowly position that Aristotle, Rousseau *et al.* assign it. The very thing that is explicitly *rejected* as a mere sub-species of language barely worthy of attention must be implicitly *re-admitted* by the back door because it is, in fact, the hidden condition of all language. This self-contradictory gesture is repeated time and time again throughout logocentric history and we will witness it in action many times in this book. In Derrida's terminology, then, we might say that the logocentric theory of the sign *deconstructs itself* and, in doing so, offers us a privileged insight to the entire edifice of 'metaphysics in deconstruction'.

What are the symptoms of this self-deconstructive movement? It is firstly revealing to note that the grammophobic history of logocentrism is actually *saturated* with images of writing albeit often in a disguised, displaced or policed form. As we will see in our discussions of Rousseau, for instance, logocentrism often does not reject writing out of hand but seeks to draw a – somewhat tenuous – distinction between 'good' and 'bad' kinds of writing. On the one hand, writing is constantly attacked as a lifeless substitute for the spoken word and – in that respect – something that inevitably leads to forgetfulness, ignorance, falsity: we start to forget things ourselves once we write them down. On the other, however, writing is often recruited to the logocentric cause so long as it remains nothing more than a faithful extension of the spoken word because – to that extent – it can prolong memory, help to transmit knowledge, truth and so on: we write things down *because* we forget them ourselves. Yet, things go further still. If western philosophy debases writing as corrupt, unreliable and so on, it is revealing to note that it regularly employs writing as a *positive* figure or metaphor for the unity, integrity and structure of the universe itself: Plato speaks of the 'divine writing' of the soul, for example, whereas medieval theology famously refers to the 'book' of God, or nature (pp. 15–18/27–31). For Derrida, it even becomes possible to describe logocentrism not as the epoch of speech but as the 'civilisation of the book', such is the ever-presence of writing within its own self-representations: 'the good writing has always been . . . enveloped in a volume or a book' (p. 18/30). In other words, logocentrism is that system of thought that seeks to *enclose* the threat of writing – its fallibility, unreliability and lack of presence – within a fixed system whose meaning is guaranteed by a pre-existing 'transcendental signified' or presence in the same way that the meaning of a book is guaranteed by its author.

In many ways, however, Derrida's single most important point about the history of logocentrism is that it is coming to a closure (p. 14/25). We are now living through what he calls the 'destruction' of the civilisation of the book (p. 18/31). It is extremely important to grasp exactly what he means by this – much misunderstood – claim, which conjures up images of the death of literacy or print culture, on the one hand, and the beginning of some brave new world, on the other. Actually, Derrida goes out of his way to make clear that proclaiming the 'closure' of logocentrism is not the same as saying that it has now come to an historical 'end' or conclusion. On the contrary: he is happy to admit that – far from being over – logocentrism may in fact continue indefinitely.[5] To be more precise, Derrida's argument is simply that we are now in a position to trace the conceptual limits or finitude of the metaphysical system: we can locate 'the crevice through which the yet unnameable glimmer beyond the closure' might be glimpsed (p. 14/25–6). Yet, why are we now in a position to draw metaphysics to a closure, if not an end, after some 2,500 years? First of all, Derrida argues that the logocentric theory of the sign as the sign *of* some pre-existent and unmediated signified – whether it be the mind of god or merely our own thoughts and feelings – has become unsustainable. What has brought us to this pass is nothing other than the uncontrollable or irrepressible position of writing within the logocentric model of signification. To look for writing within the system of logocentrism is, as we have seen, to encounter little more than a secondary or derivative medium that, at best, merely supplements the spoken word. If even the spoken word is characterised by this insurmountable state of mediation, however, then we might venture that that *all* language has the characteristics of 'writing'. For Derrida, as we will see in the next section, *every* signifier can be seen as a mere 'a signifier of a signifier' – to quote the famous logocentric dismissal of writing – as opposed to something that relates directly to a present signified: what we call 'writing' is another name for the original condition of language as a whole (p. 7/16). Finally, then, it becomes clear that what enables us to 'close the book' on logocentrism is this recognition of the inescapably mediated status of *all* signs: we cannot gain access to a full or present signified, meaning or *logos*. The 'death' of the civilisation of the book, then, signifies the growing awareness that writing cannot be traced back to a pure or unmediated presence, in the way that we can trace the words of a book back to the author who wrote them. This new concept of writing, and indeed language as a whole, has been emerging for a long time, Derrida argues, but it is now beginning to manifest itself in the form of a series of contemporary developments in post-war philosophy, science and thought (p. 6/15–16). Enter grammatology.

The Beginning of Writing

Finally, then, Derrida's brief history of logocentrism concludes with the emergence of this new concept of writing in the post-war period. It is very tempting to conclude from Derrida's survey of the last 2,500 years that *we have never had* a concept of 'writing' as such: the written word has never been considered as anything more than a poor relation or sub-species of language in general. Apparently, though, all this is about to change: what characterises the post-war period is a revolution in thought, science and technology that enables us to glimpse a radical new idea of a *generalised* and *autonomous* writing. To quickly summarise his hypothesis, Derrida proposes that writing is no longer being seen as a mere set of empirical marks or inscriptions but something much bigger: it is the condition of possibility of empirical writing, of language in general and perhaps even of our perception of the world *beyond* language. We are living through a revolution in media, computing and information technology that is in the process of transforming our understanding of language, culture and the whole sphere of human activity. If other media theorists such as Marshall McLuhan were inspired by emerging technologies because of what they tell us about the future, though, it is fair to say that Derrida is interested in what they reveal about a much more deep-rooted philosophical problematic, namely the essential nature of language itself. For Derrida, the 'beginning' of writing is not simply a historical or sociological phenomenon that happens to take place in the mid-twentieth century but nothing less than the outworking of something that has *always* been the structural condition of all linguistic signs: language has always been a form of 'writing' even if that fact is only now becoming clear. In this sense, the idea of the 'beginning' of writing is no more a simple historical event than the 'end' of the book. Why, though, does Derrida still place so much emphasis on the contemporary epoch in his history of logocentrism?

The Linguistic Turn

It is the so-called 'linguistic turn' in twentieth century philosophy, Derrida argues, that lays the groundwork for the emergence of the new science of 'grammatology' (p. 6/16). As Richard Rorty has suggested in a seminal collection of essays, what characterises twentieth century philosophy – notwithstanding all the differences between such massive figures as, say, Wittgenstein and Heidegger – is a new attention to the role of *language* within thought. To Rorty's way of thinking, language is no longer just a *tool* or medium that human beings use to describe phenomena that exist in the world outside language: a word like 'table' does not merely name the wooden structure at which I write. On the contrary, language is a defining *condition* of everything that we understand as constituting the sphere of the human: consciousness, thought, expression, culture.[6] Martin Heidegger, for instance, famously argues that it is language that 'speaks' man – rather than the other way around – in the sense that it names or calls into existence the things that constitute the world of *Dasein*.[7] Now, this concept of language as something that does not merely describe the world, but actively *constructs* the way in which we experience it, is intensified by the structuralist revolution. For Ferdinand de Saussure, linguistic signs give shape and clarity to what would otherwise be a shadowy flux of impressions in the same way that a pair of glasses gives definition to the sight of a myopic person: it is only because I have the sign of a 'table' – both the signifier and the idea or concept signified by it – that I am able to make sense of the real, actual object in front of me. If Saussure is concerned with how language mediates or constructs our experience of the real world, his structuralist successors go on to extend his principles from language to reality itself: our engagement with the real world *itself* – the world that supposedly lies beyond language – is structured according to models of signification drawn from Saussure's linguistics. In this sense, it becomes possible to speak quite seriously of the 'language' of culture (Lévi-Strauss), of the 'signifying structure' of the unconscious (Lacan), and the 'deep grammar' that is hard-wired into conscious-ness: language goes all the way down.

The Scriptural Turn

For Derrida, however, this 'linguistic' turn is in the process of being superseded by what we might call a 'scriptural' turn. It is now *writing*, and not language in general, that has become the dominant means of explaining consciousness, culture, the psyche and so on: '[n]ow we tend to say "writing" for all that and more' (p. 9/19). At the time he was preparing the *Grammatology*, Derrida was able to observe any number of instances of this 'scriptural turn' not simply within philos-ophy, or the human sciences, but in the fields of the life and cognitive sciences. First of all, he briefly alludes to the massive revolution that had taken place in the science of molecular biology over the previous decade: Watson and Crick famously speak of the structure of human DNA – the information that is built into every living cell – as a gen-etic 'code' or script (p. 9/19). Second, Derrida mentions another recent development in science: the emergence of cybernetic theory. Following the Second World War, Norbert Wiener and other theorists began to map the complex systems of information relay at work in organic bodies, machine automatons and social networks: information shuttles around loops that feed back on themselves. However, what interests Derrida is that, once more, the kind of systems, circuits and loops described by Wiener are structured – quite literally pro-*grammed* – by a generalised writing or inscription (p. 9/19). Finally, Derrida also alludes to the fact that theoretical mathematics invokes a concept of writing that exists quite independently of the spoken word: Hegel distrusted the kind of abstract mathematical symbols deployed by Leibniz, for example, precisely because they were a species of non-phonetic writing (p. 9–10/19–20). If a 'scriptural turn' was becoming visible in the mid-1960s, we might add that it is still more obvious today: Derrida refers briefly to analogue phonographic recording in his survey but we need only think of the digital revolution – where sound and light waves can be readily converted into binary code or text and back again – to see another everyday example of a 'writing' freed from the shackles of speech. In all these ways, Derrida's philosophy is in dialogue not simply with the history of philosophy but with absolutely contemporary developments.

The Beginning of Writing

What, though, is the significance of this new scriptural turn within contemporary thought for Derrida's own argument? Once again, we must stress that, in a certain sense, Derrida does not see anything absolutely *new* taking place within the contemporary revolutions in the social, life and cognitive sciences. After all, every one of them depends upon, and preserves within themselves, a very ancient idea indeed in order to make their radical discoveries intelligible: writing! On the contrary, what interests Derrida about the contemporary scriptural turn is what it tells us about the history, meaning and essence of writing itself: the fact that the term 'writing' can be applied in such a radically general and autonomous way to all manner of fields is a symptom that it is more complex than the history of logo-centrism allows. Put differently, Derrida's focus on the scriptural turn is precisely because of the insight it affords us into logocentrism in *deconstruction*: he is showing the contingency or limitations of logocen-trism's historical self-construction – the story it tells us about life, thought and history – and its capacity to be reconstructed along rad-ically different, unfamiliar lines. We already know what logocentrism thinks of writing: it is a supplement, a derivative, a mere signifier of a spoken signifier rather than something that has a direct relation to thought. If logocentrism historically presents writing as a mere sub-species of spoken language, though, molecular biology's discovery of forms of writing, code or programmes that are built into the very structure of life itself, for instance, turns this scenario on its head: it is now *language* that is a sub-species of this more general and funda-mental concept of *writing* rather than the other way around. For Derrida, the science of grammatology casts an entirely different light on the story of the last 2,500 years where a new concept of writing takes centre stage: what we have been calling the scriptural turn within the history of *language* might more accurately be described as a linguistic turn within the history of *writing* (p. 8 / 18). In other words, we might say that the 'beginning' of writing is not a new event in the history of language but something that has been inscribed within it from the start: language was always already 'writing'.

Originary Writing

The first chapter of the *Grammatology* announces a very different concept of 'writing' to the one we have learnt from the history of metaphysics, then, and the remainder of the book will flesh out this concept in more depth. It is now that Derrida begins to use the somewhat paradoxical phrase 'originary writing' (*arche-écriture*) to describe this new idea of the written word. As we will see, 'originary' writing is not the same as 'writing' in the traditional or common-sense definition of that term: what is being described here is no longer merely a set of graphic marks or inscriptions (like the words on this page) but a larger field of force that encompasses language, culture and even our experience of 'reality' itself. Yet, what exactly is 'originary' about this originary writing? To recall Derrida's opening hypothesis, what we call 'writing' describes the originary condition of language as a whole: all linguistic signs, both spoken and written, possess the characteristics that are historically attributed to writing alone. Of course, we need to stress once again here that Derrida is not making a chronological claim but a logical one: the point is not that writing historically preceded speech, but that speech possesses the same properties as writing. If historians of language habitually see 'writing' as merely a historical derivation of the spoken word – the signifier of a spoken signifier – we now know that Derrida's argument is going to be that this secondary status could in fact be applied to *all* signifiers whether spoken or written. For Derrida, as we will see in the chapters that follow, this has important implications not just for our understanding of language but for our understanding of the 'outside' world – the world of supposedly pure presence – to which language supposedly refers. Perhaps most radically of all, Derrida is going to argue that a certain idea of 'writing' is not simply a linguistic condition but rather approaches the status of something like an *ontological* condition: what we understand as consciousness, culture and (if molecular biology is to be believed) even the very building blocks of life itself are structured according to the principles of mediation, difference and relation that for the last two millennia have been synonymous with 'writing' alone. In this sense, too, we cannot see writing as something that arrives on the scene *after* an original state – speech, nature or presence – because it is already *there* at the origin itself. What does it mean, though, to say that writing is 'originary'?

Writing has no Origin

This concept of 'originary writing' actually forces us to re-think exactly what we understand by an origin. It is this aspect of Derrida's thought that is perhaps the most difficult for new readers to grasp because it strikes at one of the fundamental tenets of western thought. As we have seen, writing is not something that *befalls* a pure and immediate point of origin after the fact, it is *already there* at the origin itself. However, what does it mean to say that something so essentially secondary as writing, something that is almost impossible to think as anything other than an adjunct to something more natural or authentic, is actually originary, primary? To put it simply, Derrida's concept of an 'originary writing' is not an attempt to establish a new point of origin – as if it would be plausible to say that writing really did evolve before speech – but a way of calling into question the very idea of an origin, an absolute beginning, a pure historical, theological or philosophical point of 'presence' to which everything can be traced back. For Derrida, what is fascinating about contemporary sciences like cybernetics is the way in which 'writing' is used to name something that complicates the binary oppositions or hierarchies of value on which metaphysics seeks to institute its concept of an original presence: cybernetic theory, for instance, describes elementary information systems that take place at such a basic level that they cannot, strictly speaking, be called either human or inhuman, organic or inorganic, natural or technological (p. 9/19). If cybernetics and other grammatologies install a certain concept of writing at the very origin of language, meaning and even life, however, this origin cannot be reduced to a simple ground or presence – a single point – because it is actually an originary state of relation or complexity: 'an element without simplicity'(p. 9/19). To ask where a cybernetic system begins, for instance, is to make what philosophers call a kind of category mistake. The cybernetic circuit is an originary complex, a feedback loop, that does not begin or end anywhere but endlessly shuttles information around. This relational or differential structure – where meaning works through the *interplay* of the various elements of a system rather than by referring to something 'outside' that system – is, we will see in the next section, analogous to Derrida's own ideas on the way in which language operates.[8] In this sense, we might say that what Derrida calls the 'beginning of writing' is another way of saying that there is no such thing as a 'beginning', and we will pursue the implications of this insight in the remainder of this book.

Conclusion

What, then, has Derrida accomplished in this opening chapter of the *Grammatology*? It will be apparent that he has done little more than define the historical, cultural and philosophical field of his enquiry. At this early stage, he is still in the process of articulating his own position and what form it will and will not take. To reiterate his argument, Derrida's vision of the 'beginning of writing' does not herald some brave new world beyond the illusions of metaphysics, but a more modest and ultimately more rigorous attempt to demarcate the conceptual limits of the logocentric theory of the sign and, with it, the enclosure of metaphysics as a whole. Once again, it is not a question of rejecting this theory or the logocentric tradition more generally: 'nothing is conceivable for us without them' (p. 13/25). To reject logocentrism is to reject the possibility of thought itself. For Derrida, it is only by working and thinking through this tradition that we can begin to call it into question: we must use the language of metaphysics *and* cross it out, preserve it *and* erase it at the same time. If we cannot simply demolish the logocentric theory of the sign – and all the assumptions about the signifier and the signified, the primary and the secondary, the spoken and the written that it contains – what we can do is question its self-construction, construct it differently, in short, *deconstruct* it. What is the essence of writing? Is it merely a secondary supplement to speech or does it perform a more essential, even constitutive role? To what extent do we need to construct what Derrida calls a 'new logic' of this supposed supplement? (p. 7/17). In the second chapter of the *Grammatology*, Derrida moves on to give more detailed answers to these questions via a famous close reading of the work of Ferdinand de Saussure.

Saussure, Writing and the Trace

What exactly *is* 'grammatology'? It is this question that Derrida's book now seeks to address. As we saw in the previous section, the western philosophical tradition has never produced a genuine science of *writing* as such. From Plato to Rousseau, the written word has always been seen as little more than a sub-species of speech. Yet, what recent developments within the life, cognitive and human sciences have revealed is a generalised concept of writing, existing entirely independently of speech, which makes a mockery of such 'historico-metaphysical' presuppositions (*Grammatology*, p. 27/42). To Derrida's way of thinking, then, it now becomes essential to ask what kind of science might do justice to this new concept of writing: could we construct a 'general grammatology' to describe this general writing (p. 30/45)? If the first chapter of the book is concerned with delineating the field for an inquiry, the task is now to try to establish a theoretical framework and vocabulary with which to describe that field. For Derrida, it is here that the central questions that drive *Of Grammatology* begin to be posed. What form, if any, should a new science of writing take? Is it, for example, a historical, anthropological, linguistic or philosophical project? Perhaps most importantly, to what extent is it even *possible* to construct a science of something that, as we saw in the previous section, seems to be the condition not simply of language in general but of any complex system or structure? In this chapter, we will see that grammatology – the science of writing – cannot be a science like any other because writing calls into question the very possibility of science itself.

Grammatology

First, Derrida offers a brief account of previous attempts to construct a science of writing. As we have seen in the introduction, 'grammatology' in the broadest sense of the term has a long pedigree: William Warburton, for example, announces 'a general history of writing' as early as 1742 (p. 75/112). However, Derrida argues that every previous attempt to fashion a grammatology – a systematic study of the origins, nature or essence of writing – runs into an insurmountable problem. Quite simply, the very idea of a 'science of writing' puts the scientific cart before the horse: writing cannot be the *object* of a science, Derrida argues, because it is what makes scientific study *possible* in the first place. Why is this? For Derrida, as we saw in our discussion of Husserl, writing is the sole means by which we can record, preserve and transmit our thoughts and thus establish something as 'truth', 'knowledge' or 'objectivity' in the first place: the written text is what enables the objects of geometry to transcend the mind of the first geometers, for instance, and become universal objects for everyone. Now, this is the crux of the problem for any grammatology, Derrida argues. If writing is what makes scientific objectivity possible, then this means that it cannot itself be reduced to the *object* of a grammatology in the same way that, say, a living cell might be the object of biology or a piece of rock the object of geology. In other words, any genuine 'science' of writing would have to be the science of something that constitutes the very *possibility* of science itself.

The Science of Writing

It is not enough to say that every previous attempt to construct a grammatology presupposes the very thing it seeks to explain, however, because these attempts also betray a certain prejudice against writing: the logocentric hierarchy of speech over the written word. Any scientific, historical or anthropological enquiry into writing – however objective or impartial it may claim to be – already contains a certain pre-understanding of the very thing it is attempting to discover. To be sure, every would-be grammatologist always begins by asking the basic and fundamental question 'what is writing?'. Unfortunately, the problem is that they generally presume a certain kind of answer to that question too. For Derrida, what is striking about the history of grammatology is that any inquiry into the *essence* of writing is quickly set to one side – as if the answer were self-evident – in favour of a historical inquiry into the *origins* of writing within culture. What is important is not *what* writing is, in other words, but *when* it came into being. If we examine any history of writing from Warburton onwards, for example, it is striking that the conclusions they reach are largely the same: everyone automatically assumes that (a) speech is the primary form of language (b) writing is nothing more than a derivation of speech and so (c) writing in its purest form is thus phonetic and, more precisely, alphabetic. In Derrida's account, there are good reasons for asking whether this so-called 'science' of writing may in fact be the product of an entirely metaphysical set of assumptions.

Linguistics

In summary, then, Derrida's goal is to consider whether it is possible to construct a new 'science' of writing. It is the field of contemporary linguistics, and particularly the work of the 'father' of structuralism Ferdinand de Saussure, that provides him with his initial point of departure. But why linguistics? Of course, Derrida's decision to 'take on' Saussurean linguistics is not simply an arbitrary one. Insofar as it is a discipline that offers a scientific analysis of language itself, linguistics would seem to be in a better position than, say history, anthropology or archaeology to offer a rigorous definition of writing in general. However, there are more important historical reasons why the *Grammatology* should turn to linguistics in its quest for a science of writing. First of all, Derrida rightly observes that linguistics is not merely one science among others but arguably the 'queen' of the contemporary 'human sciences' (p. 28/44). We have already seen how Saussure's theory provides the basic model for structuralist anthropology, psychoanalysis and other disciplines: Lacan, Lévi-Strauss and other thinkers rely heavily upon his account of the sign to articulate the structure of the unconscious, culture and so on. More importantly still, however, Derrida argues that Saussure's theory of the sign plays an absolutely decisive role in problematising the logocentric theory of the sign as nothing more than the physical representation *of* some pre-existing idea or concept (*Positions*, p. 18). For Saussure, as we will see, the signifier and the signified – the physical mark and the concept it refers to – are inextricably linked to one another like two sides of the same sheet of paper: this insight is an important step beyond the old metaphysical or theological view we saw in the previous section where ideas seem to exist wholly independently of the sounds and marks used to describe them. If Saussure's theory is ground-breaking in many ways, though, Derrida still remains somewhat sceptical of the scientific pretensions of linguistics: we will see how Saussure's most promising lines of enquiry are – just like those of structuralism more generally – prematurely closed down by a dogmatic and speculative metaphysical commitment to the value of presence (*Grammatology*, p. 46/67). What, then, is Derrida's reading of Saussure?

From Linguistics to Grammatology

I would now like to consider Derrida's famous and extremely detailed reading of Saussure's linguistic theory in the chapter 'Linguistics and Grammatology'. We will concentrate purely on what Derrida has to say about Saussure himself (and put to one side his very interesting comments on other linguists such as Jakobson, Peirce or Hjelmslev) in order to be as clear as possible. As we'll see, Saussure seeks to offer nothing less than a general science of language itself but Derrida will argue that this science is neither particularly general nor even very scientific. To start with, Saussure's method is (at least declaredly) 'phonological': it sees *sound structures*, in other words, as the basis of all language including writing: what is intended to be an objective science of language as a whole thus begins by reproducing the classic hierarchy of speech over writing. If Saussure's linguistic theory is an obvious target for a deconstructive reading, however, Derrida's working method is not to subject it to an external critique but, once again, to tease out the immanent contradictions within it: Saussure manages to *both* declare a preference for speech *and*, as we will see, to articulate a radical new concept of writing as the condition of language per se. In Derrida's view, Saussure's linguistics, for all its weaknesses, still succeeds in offers us a tantalising glimpse of a 'general grammatology' (p. 30/45) from within the logocentric enclosure of linguistics.

Ferdinand de Saussure's *Course in General Linguistics* (*Cours de linguistique générale*) is generally seen as a ground-breaking text within linguistics and the foundation of the new science of structuralism. It introduces a number of radical innovations in the study of language.

First, Saussure argues that the object of linguistics is what he calls '*la langue*': the underlying structure of language as a whole as opposed to specific speech acts or utterances (*la parole*). As we saw earlier, this move from the specific to the general or systematic prepares the ground for the structuralist revolution.

According to Saussure's structure-based approach, language is not a nomenclature, that is, a series of names for pre-existing objects in the outside world. On the contrary, it is a system that acquires meaning through its own internal structure and relations. For Saussure, it is possible to break down any linguistic sign into two intrinsically linked components. On the one hand, there is the *signifier*, or what he terms the 'sound image'. On the other, there is the *signified*, or concept, to which that signifier refers. In Saussure's view, however, both signifier and signified must be distinguished from what he calls the *referent*: any real thing in the external world beyond language.

To introduce another important point, however, Saussure argues that the relation between any given signifier and signified is *arbitrary*. It is motivated by tradition or convention, in other words, rather than by any perceived 'natural resemblance' between sound and concept. If I use the sound 'cat' to refer to the concept of a cat, it is not because there is any natural relation between this particular signifier and signified but rather because it is accepted that the two go together within the conventions of the English language: the convention is very different in the French and Italian languages, for instance, where other signifiers ('chat' or 'gatto') relate to the signified.

Finally, and most importantly, however, Saussure also argues that any linguistic sign only acquires its meaning through its *difference* from other linguistic signs rather than through any 'positive' value it might possess in itself. The meaning of any sign is determined by its difference – both phonic and conceptual – from other signs within the system. This complex linguistic system – arbitrary, conventional and differential – is the basis for our experience of the world outside language. In Saussure's view, it is only through such linguistic signs that we can articulate, or make sense of, the world beyond language: the sign of a cat – both sound and concept – is what makes it possible for us to process the flux of sensations and impressions that comprise my experience of the world.

Speech
To begin with, Derrida shows the ways in which Saussure's science of language is still governed by the logic of inclusion and exclusion that characterises logocentrism: speech/writing, inside/outside, intelligible/sensible, natural/unnatural and so on. First, Saussure's phonological bias quickly leads him to the conclusion that it is speech, rather than writing, that is the essential mode of the linguistic sign. It is only the spoken signifier, in other words, that refers to the signified

(p. 30/45). As we have suggested above, Saussure is the great theorist of the 'arbitrariness' of the sign: no signifier possesses a natural relationship with a signified. Yet, this does not stop him canvassing for just this natural proximity of speech and sense (*Course in General Linguistics*, p. 32). Second, and following on from this, Saussure goes on to relegate writing to a secondary or derivative position that is external to the inner system of language. Once again, writing is seen in purely phonetic terms: it is nothing but the signifier of a originary spoken signifier, as opposed to something that possesses a direct relation to its signified. For Saussure, revealingly, writing does not merely stand outside the essential structure of language but outside the state of nature in which speech and meaning reside together: the written word has the 'exteriority' of 'a dangerous, almost maleficent technique' Derrida says (p. 34/51). Finally, then, Derrida concludes that – for all its apparent scientific rigour – Saussure's theory ends up reproducing the most traditional logocentric gestures imaginable. On the one hand, speech is identified with nature, presence and, more generally, the 'inside' of language. On the other, writing is equated with the unnatural, with the absent or mediated and with the 'outside' of the linguistic system. If Saussure purports to offer a 'science of writing', though, the question is whether this deeply metaphysical framework is going to be up to the task of articulating the radically new and generalised writing we have been tracing. To what extent, then, does Saussure's grammatology stand up?

The Return of Writing

As Derrida goes on to show, the cracks begin to appear almost immediately in the edifice of Saussure's argument. It is revealing, for starters, just how much space the latter devotes to discussing writing in the *Course* given its supposedly marginal place within the linguistic schema as a whole. Why bother speaking about it at all if it is so unimportant (p. 34/51)? Quite simply, Derrida suspects that Saussure dedicates so much time to writing because he perceives it as a *threat* to his speech-centred model of linguistics: what was supposed to be external to the system of language now seemingly endangers that system at its very core. Saussure even goes on to denounce writing in what are – for a supposedly objective study – exceptionally emotive, violent or hysterical terms: the written word is deemed to be treacherous, monstrous, and even tyrannical. Intriguingly, he is especially worried that writing may displace speech from its position at the centre of language and reverse the natural order of the spoken and the written word. What concerns him is that the written word – because it seems to represent a more durable, lasting mode of signification than speech – will gradually come to be seen as representative of language as a whole. Now, this would be an absolute disaster, in his view, because writing mediates, or even breaks, what he sees as the 'natural bond' between sound and sense. If writing is taken to represent language as whole, Saussure predicts, all sorts of apocalyptic catastrophes will ensue. The spelling of a word will come to influence, and even modify, the way in which that word is said, he says, and even in his own time this is leading to terrible mispronunciations. This scenario will not strike many readers as particularly awful though – is mispronunciation really such a disaster? (p. 41/61–2) – and so we might be tempted to wonder why it is clearly so important to Saussure. For Derrida, Saussure's hysterical venom in attacking what are, after all, fairly banal or everyday changes in language is once again indicative of the extent to which this supposed science of language seems to contain a larger metaphysical agenda (p. 41/61–2). In Saussure's account, it often appears that writing is not merely a linguistic threat but a *moral* one: the written word turns the natural order of things upside down (p. 34/51).

Writing at the Origin
What, then, is really going on here? It is clear that Saussure's attempt to posit speech as the natural essence of language is beginning to fall apart under the threat of writing but what we need to understand is *why* this state of affairs takes place. As we have just seen, Saussure denounces the arrival of writing into language as a kind of unnatural accident or catastrophe that befalls what was until then a pure state of nature where speech and sense lived happily together: writing arrives like Satan into the Garden of Eden, and Adam and Eve are cast out. However, this kind of quasi-religious or mythological narrative of a fall from some prelapsarian innocence actually explains nothing at all. To introduce what will be his own explanation, Derrida contends that the threat embodied by writing is not something that befalls language from the 'outside', so to speak, but the original state of language itself: ' "Usurpation" has always

already begun' (p. 37/55). We will spend the rest of this chapter, indeed the remainder of this book, unpacking this radical but paradoxical claim. For Derrida, what appears to be an external *threat to* the purity of language – the danger represented by writing, difference and mediation – is nothing less than the original, and thus impure, *condition* of language as a whole. If Saussure's commitment to logocentrism stands on unstable foundations, then this instability reveals itself in the 'contradictory logic' that plagues his own text. On the one hand, we have seen that Saussure argues for the *natural* priority of speech over writing and, in this respect, his theory of language remains wholly logocentric. On the other, however, we will now see that Saussure also insists upon the arbitrary, conventional and differential – that is *non-natural* – status of *all* linguistic signs and, in this sense, his linguistic theory appears to open the door to a more radical concept of writing. Which Saussure, then, are we to believe? How does the theorist of the arbitrary (non-natural) status of every linguistic sign still manage to argue for the natural priority of speech? To what extent, more importantly, can his attempt to dismiss writing as the 'mere signifier of a signifier' be squared with his larger argument about the essentially *differential* status of *all* language, whereby *every* sign works by referring to *other* signs within the system?

Arche-writing

Third, then, I want to show how Derrida uses Saussure's theory to articulate a radically new and generalised concept of writing. His aim is to pursue what we might call the logical trajectory of Saussure's argument to its utmost conclusions: Saussure does not always recognise – or want to recognise – the radical nature of his own argument. Upon Derrida's analysis, it is very revealing that Saussure constantly invokes 'writing' as a kind of metaphor or analogy to describe general linguistic conditions: what is supposedly a limited or derivative form of language increasingly, and contrary to his own express intentions, becomes the name for language as whole (p. 52/75–7). For Derrida, Saussure increasingly goes beyond the residually metaphysical perimeters of his linguistic theory to establish the basis for a 'general' science of writing or grammatology. If Saussure's text explicitly seeks to relegate writing to the margins, Derrida identifies a number of key moments where the written word breaks through to the heart of his linguistic system: his thesis of the arbitrary nature of the relation between the signifier and the signified, his argument that the signifier is primarily differential rather than phonic and, most radically, his articulation of an originary 'trace' or writing that precedes the oppositions between speech and writing. In Derrida's view, Saussure's turn to writing is less an accident or an unwitting contradiction than the *return* of something he is constantly trying to repress: generalised 'writing' is the true basis of linguistics.

The arbitrariness of the sign

To start with, Derrida examines Saussure's famous thesis of the arbitrary nature of the sign. As we know, Saussure's contention is that that there is a 'natural bond' between the phonic signifier and the signified – sound and sense – which the written word cannot enter into. Earlier, however, we also saw how he argues that all linguistic signs are *arbitrary*: any relation between a given signifier and a given signified is the product of convention – culture, tradition, rules – as opposed to, say, a natural resemblance between the two. We can thus see an obvious contradiction in Saussure's logic that unsettles his claim about the natural priority of speech over writing. Either there is a natural relation between the spoken signifier and the signified or no sign has a natural relation to what it signifies. Both cannot be true![9] Now, if the thesis of the arbitrariness of the sign contradicts Saussure's claim about the natural priority of speech, it also calls into question his argument about the inferiority of writing. For Saussure, as we have seen, speech is natural whereas writing is the unnatural, technical or artificial inscription of the spoken word in permanent graphic form. If all linguistic signs are now deemed to be arbitrary, however, then this means that *all* language has the unnatural status that Saussure attempts to attribute to writing alone. In other words, all language – both spoken and written signs – properly belongs to the category that Saussure names 'writing'.

The differential nature of language

According to Derrida, however, it is another of Saussure's major insights that best enables us to see the 'written' character of all language: 'language', the linguist argues, consists of a series of 'differences *without positive terms*' (*Course*, pp. 117–18). It is with this claim that we approach the true originality of Saussure's theory of the sign but we need to go slowly to understand what is at stake here. First, Saussure prepares the ground for his big idea by suddenly announcing that the phonic or spoken signifier is *not* actually defined by its relation to sound after all. Saussure goes on to perform what we might call a kind of phenomenological 'reduction' of the phonic signifier: what is important is how that signifier presents itself to our consciousness, he says, rather than any relation it might possess to an actual sound. We must recognise that the sign is first and foremost a *psychic* phenomenon, in other words, in the sense that it exists independently of its *physical* embodiment in sound when spoken: 'the linguistic signifier . . . is not phonic but incorporeal – constituted not by its material substance' (pp. 118–19).[10] Now, we should once again note that this attempt to argue that there is nothing *essentially* phonic about the sign contradicts Saussure's theory of the 'natural' bond between sound and sense. However, it also raises a further and more pressing question: if signifiers do not acquire meaning from real or physical sounds, where *do* they get their significance from? For Saussure, the answer to this question is that a sign actually acquires meaning through its *difference* from *other* signs:

Whether we take the signified or the signifier, language has neither ideas nor sounds that existed before the linguistic system, but only conceptual and phonic differences that have issued from the system. The idea or phonic substance that a sign contains is of less importance than the other signs that surround it. (*Course*, pp. 117–18)

What exactly is Saussure saying here? If any one sign has meaning, it is not because it possesses any content or substance in itself but because it *differs* – both phonically and conceptually – from other signs within the linguistic system. The sign 'cat' (regardless of whether we see it from the perspective of the sound *or* the concept) exists within a prior network of relations to *other* signs ('hat', 'bat' and so on). There is a paradoxical sense in which the idea of a singular or unique sign is, then, something of a contradiction-in-terms. This is because any apparently singular, 'present' and independent sign necessarily contains within it the *traces* of other signs within the system against which it is to be defined. In Derrida's view, as we will see in a moment, this theory has radical implications for the logo-centric theory of the sign.

Language is Writing

We now come to one of the most important aspects of Derrida's reading of Saussure. It is once again revealing, Derrida notes, that Saussure increasingly turns to *writing* as an explanatory model for his differential theory of language: 'we shall use writing to draw some comparisons that will clarify the whole issue' (*Course*, p. 165). Unfortunately, the analogy with writing clarifies 'the whole issue' in a way that Saussure himself presumably never intended. Earlier, we saw how he dismisses writing in very traditional terms as nothing more than a 'signifier of a signifier': the written word refers only to the spoken word and has no direct or natural access to the signified itself. However, any attempt to establish a natural priority of speech over writing obviously cannot be sustained in the light of the larger argument that language depends upon a series of differences as opposed to any positive substance. Quite simply, we cannot speak or hear 'difference' as such: what enables us to tell one sound from another – the difference between them – is not itself a sound. To embrace difference as the key to the entire system of language is thus to bid farewell to any privilege that speech may once have possessed. For Saussure, then, it becomes impossible to sustain the natural priority of speech and this may be why he increasingly turns to writing as a metaphor or analogy for the workings of language as a whole (*Grammatology*, p. 53/77). If writing is merely a 'signifier of a signifier' that never possesses a direct or essential relation to meaning, then perhaps it actually offers a better insight than speech into the differential status of language itself. The fact is that *every* signifier might best be described as a 'signifier of a signifier' because, according to Saussure's own theory, every sign works by referring to other signs within the system rather than to some positive content of its own. There is an important sense, then, in which the lowly position of writing – inferior, derivative, always at one step removed from the main action – accurately describes the position of language as a whole. This means that writing is not so much 'comparable' to language as the other way around: language might even be described as a species *of* writing (p. 52/75). In this sense, Saussure begins to articulate one of the most important, if paradoxical, ideas in Derrida's theoretical vocabulary: *arche-* or *originary* writing (*arche-écriture*).

'Arche-*writing*'

Why, to conclude, does Derrida choose this specific term '*arche*-writing' to explain the complex phenomenon he is describing? It is very important to be clear about what he means by this complex and much-misunderstood expression. As we have already suggested on a number of occasions, 'originary writing' is not an attempt to literally reverse the hierarchy of speech over writing: Derrida is not suggesting that children learn to write before they talk, that written culture precedes oral culture, that writing is somehow 'better' than speech. To be absolutely precise, Derrida's contention is that the position historically attributed to 'writing' in western culture actually describes the condition of all language whatsoever: what is called 'writing' names the framework 'common to all systems of signification' (p. 46/68) whether they be spoken, written, drawn, electronically recorded or transmitted. Indeed, he goes to great pains to distinguish this 'originary' concept of writing from what he calls the 'vulgar' or conventional idea of writing as a set of empirical marks, letters or inscriptions (p. 46/68). Yet, if '*arche*-writing' is not 'writing' in the common-sense definition of the term, then why not clear up any possibility of confusion by dispensing with this 'vulgar' name altogether and inventing some new and less prejudicial way of talking about it? For Derrida, as we have already seen, this new language is a stark impossibility: we are compelled to borrow 'under erasure' the vocabulary of metaphysics – speech, writing, sign, presence – even when it is that vocabulary that we wish to call into question because there is nothing else. If we cannot invent a new language, Derrida also supplies a more precise reason why he retains – cautiously, critically and strategically – the name of 'writing'. The new concept of *arche*-writing 'essentially communicates' with the vulgar concept of writing in the same kind of way that, for Freudian psychoanalysis, unconscious desire communicates with its visible, manifest form. This vulgar or traditional concept of writing as the mere signifier of a signifier constitutes, in other words, the repressed, displaced or disguised truth of the state of language as a whole (p. 56/83). In Derrida's account, that is, it is not a question of dispensing with this vulgar concept so much as *turning it inside out* in order to reveal what lies repressed within it: the general state of mediation that he calls *arche*-writing.

The Originary Trace

Finally, and most importantly, then, I want to move on from the specific question of speech versus writing to consider the most far-reaching implication of Derrida's reading of Saussure: the concept of an 'originary trace'. This is arguably the single most important idea in the *Grammatology* and the basis of Derrida's deconstruction of metaphysics more generally. As we have already begun to see, deconstruction turns on revealing a certain quality of mediation, difference or relation at the heart of every supposed 'presence': speech, consciousness and so on. To put it simply, what Derrida calls the originary trace represents his most systematic attempt to articulate this central point in the *Grammatology*: mediation goes all the way down. For Derrida, as we will see, this concept complicates not simply the opposition between speech and writing but every opposition that goes to make up the metaphysics of presence: the intelligible and the sensible, the transcendental and the empirical, and so on *ad infinitum*. In each case, we will see how every 'present' term, ground or value depends for its identity upon the trace of other values that are never themselves simply present.

The Trace

What, then, *is* the 'originary trace'? We need to go back to Saussure's own linguistic theory in order to answer this question. Earlier, we saw how, almost despite himself, Saussure argues that difference is the original condition of possibility of all meaning. To recall Saussure's argument, linguistic signs are not constituted by any intrinsic phonic or conceptual substance – a particular sound or idea that is inherent to that sign itself – but by their *difference* from other signs in the system. If every sign in the system obtains its identity through its difference from all the other signs, then this means every sign is intrinsically marked by what it is not. Every sign must retain the *traces* of the other signs against which it is to be defined, in other words, in order to have any meaning at all. The essential or constitutive process by which every sign is related to every other is what Derrida means by the 'originary trace'. This originary or constitutive 'trace' that inhabits every sign has, as we will see, important implications for our understanding of presence. For Saussure, no sign is ever simply 'present' in time or space – whereby it exists in, or refers only to, itself – because it cannot function without implicitly referring to other signs which are, thus, not simply spatially or temporally 'absent' either. In this sense, we might conclude that every sign is stratified – spaced out – in the sense that its meaning is always dependent on the traces of other signs that differ from it in both space and time.

The Trace is Différance

We now encounter another very important term in Derrida's vocabulary that will need to be carefully unpacked. To clarify his position, Derrida suddenly introduces what is now one of his most famous – or notorious – concepts into the discussion: '*the (pure) trace*' he declares, is *différance* [*la trace (pure) et la différance*]' (p. 62/92). What exactly, though, does this complex claim mean?

1. First, we need to understand what Derrida means by '*différance*' itself.[11] Unfortunately, he offers no clear definition of the term in the *Grammatology* so we have to look elsewhere. In *Speech and Phenomena*, for example, he says this: '[w]e shall designate by the term *différance* the movement by which any language, or any code, any system of reference in general, becomes "historically" constituted as a fabric of differences' (p. 141).

2. What kind of 'movement' are we talking about here? For Derrida, it is important to recognise that 'différance' is a neologism – a newly coined term – that brings together two subtly different senses of the French verb '*différer*'. On the one hand, it means 'to differ' (in the sense of distinguishing or differentiating something from something else). On the other, it means to 'to defer' (in the sense of delaying or postponing something to a later point in time).

3. If '*différance*' refers to a process of 'differing/deferring', then, we need to consider what this means in the context of Saussure's theory of the sign. On the one hand, it signifies the way in which any sign is extended or spread out across space in the sense that its identity necessarily refers to other elements that exist alongside it in the system. On the other, it connotes the way in which any sign is deferred

or postponed in time in the sense that its identity always refers to elements that exist before or after it in the linguistic system.

For Derrida, what is called *'différance'* has extremely important implications for Saussure's theory of language and the logocentric concept of the sign more generally. If the identity of *every* sign depends upon this spatio-temporal trace of *other* signs, then, *contra* Saussure, this has radical consequences for the traditional idea of the sign as something that stands in for, and makes present, a prior meaning. In Derrida's rival account, language works through a process of infinite supplementation where the job of completing or fulfilling meaning is always devolved onto the *next* sign along in space and time: a fully present meaning is thus perpetually out of reach.

The Deconstruction of the Sign
Let's take this slowly. It is Derrida's argument, remember, that logocentrism always sees the sign as the sign *of* something: Aristotle, for example, saw language as the physical representation of a pre-existing idea that is present to our consciousness. Indeed, we might argue that this gesture survives all the way up to Saussure's distinction between the signifier and the signified: every sound or graphic mark still refers to a given idea or concept even if, for Saussure, that relation is now revealed to be entirely arbitrary. However, what the originary trace shows us is that every sign first refers to other signs, as opposed to some 'present' concept that is not itself a sign. We can see, then, that the originary trace throws the whole logocentric concept of the sign into crisis by proposing that we *never* arrive at a simple or unmediated meaning: nothing is unmediated. For Derrida, every signifier relates to other signifiers that surround it in space and time and so we can never reach a pure thought or concept – a signified – that exists in and of itself independently of all signifiers: what is supposedly *beyond* language is plunged back *into* language. If we take a very simple example of this, it becomes much clearer: every time we look up a word in the dictionary – 'love', for example – what we find is not the meaning of that word but merely other words that act as synonyms for it ('love' means 'adoration' or 'desire') or even antonyms ('love' means the opposite of 'hate'). Just as every time we try to find the meaning of a word in a dictionary we are referred to other words, Derrida argues,

so every time we try to establish the signified of a signifier we are led to *other signifiers*. Now, this state of affairs, where every signifier refers to other signifiers, forces us to consider exactly what we mean by the term 'signified', in the first place. The thing that Saussure persists in calling a 'signified' idea or concept must – according to the strict logic of his own theory – be merely just *another* signifier that is no more privileged than any other within the system. This is why no 'transcendental signified' we will encounter in this book – God, nature, consciousness, structure, presence – ever manages to escape the play of mutual relations, mediations and differences that constitutes language (p. 7/16). In Derrida's account, all thought remains caught with the network of spatial and temporal differentiation that is the 'trace': '*We think only in signs*' (p. 50/73, English in original).

The Deconstruction of Metaphysics

To Derrida's eyes, however, Saussure's 'originary trace' can be extended to cover not simply language but the realm of thought, consciousness and perception itself: what we like to think of as the 'pure' realm of thought is itself sucked into the process of differing/deferring that he names '*différance*'. It is Derrida's aim, that is, to push the logic of Saussure's position straight through the logocentric assumptions about speech, writing and presence in which it is still enclosed to its most radical conclusions: what begins as a scientific account of language ends up as a means of deconstructing the metaphysical worldview in its entirety. As we have just seen, Saussure's differential account of language throws the logocentric theory of the sign into crisis by insisting upon the irreducibly mediated status of all thought: we can never escape the differing and deferring network of signifiers into the realm of a pure or transcendental signified. Yet this is still only the beginning of the story for Derrida. If Derrida devotes so much time to the logocentric theory of the sign, remember, it is because it is a privileged means of access to the *entire logic* of metaphysics itself: the opposition between the signifier and the signified is a portal, so to speak, through which we can enter every other opposition that makes up the metaphysics of presence, such as the opposition between the soul and the body, the ideal and the material, the transcendental and the empirical and so forth. Just as the idea of an originary trace enables us to question the supposed 'presence' of the signified, in other words, so it also contains the seeds of a powerful critique of the presence of other privileged concepts like the soul, the ideal and the transcendental: what appears to be a pure, unmediated and present term can, in each case, be shown to acquire its definition from the traces of other elements which are, at least apparently, absent. From the apparently limited field of language, then, Derrida's analysis gradually broadens out to encompass the entire field of the metaphysics of presence. In his own words, the concept of an originary trace, where 'the absolutely other [*le tout autre*] is announced as such – without any simplicity, any identity, any resemblance or continuity – within what is not it' articulates its possibility 'in the entire field of being [*étant*], which metaphysics has defined as the being-present [*étant-présent*]' (p. 47/69, translation modified). What, then, is the impact of the trace on metaphysics as a whole?

The Origin of Metaphysics
For Derrida, what is most radical about the trace from the point of view of the metaphysics of presence is that it is *originary* (p. 65/95). It is not the trace *of* some present thing, in other words, but nothing outside the pure production of differences itself. As such, he argues, the originary trace is unthinkable within the conceptual logic of the metaphysics of presence. Let's try to cash out this claim:

1. First, Derrida argues that the trace is neither *present* nor *absent*. As Saussure himself makes clear, what the differential theory of language means is that no 'present' element in a system (something that has actually been spoken, for instance, or written down) can function without referring to other so-called 'absent' elements (something that has not been said or written). If every element bears the traces of every other element, then we can only conclude that no element is ever simply 'there' or 'not-there'.

2. According to the same logic, the trace is neither *sensible* nor *intelligible*. It is not something that can be recognised by our senses (like a sound or smell), in other words, nor something that can be conceived within our minds (like an idea or concept). On the one hand, we cannot see or hear it because, it is nothing but the difference *between* spoken or written marks. On the other, we cannot quite think it either

because, once again, the difference *between* ideas or concepts cannot, strictly speaking, *itself* be a concept (p. 62/92–3).

3. To go further still, we cannot see the trace as belonging to either the category of the *subject* or the *object*. It is neither a property of our being – like being strong or intelligent – nor something that simply happens to us from outside – like capitalism or global warming – but something that exceeds the spatial opposition between interiority and exteriority. In Derrida's readings of Husserl, for example, we saw how the supposed purity of our interior consciousness requires the traces of the 'external' world (communication, indication, writing) in order to relate to itself in the first place: what is apparently 'outside' is already 'inside' (p. 44/65).

4. For Derrida, as we will see in more detail in the next section, the originary trace also does not belong to the opposition between *nature* and *culture* or any of its corollaries (the living and the non-living, the organic and the inorganic, the natural and the technical). If the eighteenth-century philosopher Jean-Jacques Rousseau seeks to crit- icise modern civil society from the perspective of an idealised state of nature, we will see that what he calls 'nature' is not a simple, orig- inary moment of pure presence but something that *already* differs from itself. In Derrida's account, nature de-natures, or deviates from, itself even within its own supposed essence: the natural is already cultural.

5. Finally, the originary trace is neither an *empirical or historical event* nor a *transcendental cause or condition*. On the one hand, it never attains the conceptual presence – the unity, stability or simplicity – that we associate with a transcendental cause or condition: the trace will never be an equivalent to Plato's Ideas or Kant's Categories. On the other, however, it has never been nor ever will be 'present' in space and time: the trace is not a historical event or process like the Battle of Hastings or the Industrial Revolution. For Derrida, the trace cannot be traced to any point of simple spatial or temporal presence – whether a present that is now past or one that is yet to come – because it is the underlying differential condition of any 'presence' whatso- ever. In Derrida's own paradoxical phrase, the originary trace can never be 'there' because it is 'always-already-there [*toujours déjà-là*]': it both recedes into an infinite past and projects itself into an infinite future (p. 66/97).

Why, then, is it impossible to think the trace within the logic of meta-physics? In simple terms, the trace is prior to every metaphysical concept because it is the movement of *différance* – of differing and deferring – that allows them to *appear as* concepts in the first place: '[*t*]*he trace is in fact the absolute origin of sense in general*' (pp. 62/95).

Metaphysics has no Origin
Now, we still need to be clear about exactly what Derrida *means*, however, when he says that the trace is the 'origin' of metaphysics. It is very tempting to see the trace as simply the latest in a long line of ultimate causes, grounds or foundations that philosophers erect in order to explain or organise reality. As Derrida describes it, this mys-terious force occasionally resembles some master-concept like Hegel's Spirit, Heidegger's Being or even the ineffably transcendent God of Christian theology: the trace is the origin of everything but, like God, it is invisible, ineffable and even unthinkable. Yet, if the trace is indeed the *origin* of metaphysics, it is crucial to recognise that it is not a *meta-physical* point of origin, that is to say, a simple, unified or present ground on which a metaphysical theory of knowledge can establish itself. Quite simply, the whole point of the trace is that it is an orginary condition of mediation, synthesis or complexity rather than a present being, thing or entity: '[t]he trace is *nothing*, it is not an entity, it exceeds the question *What is?*' (p. 75/110). If metaphysical theories of knowl-edge generally try to explain the contingency of the world by referring everything back to a simple, unified or undivided cause – an ultimate origin – the trace forces us to try to imagine 'an originary synthesis' that is not preceded by any absolute simplicity. To declare that 'every-thing begins with the trace', then, is not an attempt to posit some new, even more fundamental point of origin, in other words, but to assert that *there is no pure, simple or present origin in the first place* (p. 65/95). For Derrida, that is to say, any origin is always multiple: what claims to be a singular point of origin must always define itself against something that it is not, dividing itself in at least two, multiplying itself like a cell through a process of infinite differing/deferring. The moment of pure or simple 'presence' upon which every metaphysical value system is founded, whether it be God or merely consciousness, is thus always shot through with differences, relations, traces of other elements. This is why the metaphysics of presence – what Derrida calls the definition

of Being as 'being-present' – can be said to reside on a grounding or foundational instability. In short, the 'origin' of the metaphysics of presence is *never* itself present.

The (im-)possibility of Metaphysics

Finally, then, we can begin to see why the originary trace is the basis for Derrida's deconstruction of the metaphysics of presence. It is the engine that drives his re-evaluation of the history, logic and institutions of western philosophy and we will see it recur in different forms (writing, *différance*, the supplement) throughout this book. As we have seen, metaphysics operates by establishing a series of binary oppositions and hierarchies whereby a superior term (speech, thought, the ideal) is identified with pure and immediate presence and an inferior term (writing, the body, the material) is equated with mediation, loss of presence, absence. However, if any apparent 'presence' must contain the traces of what is *not* simply present in order to be itself in the first place, then this oppositional logic becomes unsustainable. What should be opposed and hierarchised terms presuppose one another. To Derrida's eyes, any value that metaphysics posits as 'present' – speech, nature, consciousness – is thus always already spreading or dispersing outwards into a network of traces, differences and mediations: *nothing* is ever purely present or absent. Now, the implications of this state of affairs for the metaphysics of presence itself are massive. If difference is the secret or repressed 'origin' of all presence, then this means that the metaphysical systems of thought that are erected *upon* that illusory value of presence must be rethought from the ground up. For Derrida, in other words, we must redescribe the entire history of metaphysics as a series of more or less unsuccessful attempts to get to grips with the originary trace: 'metaphysics' is once again revealed to be 'metaphysics in deconstruction'. On the one hand, the trace is the *only* basis on which metaphysics gets going in the first place: every appeal to posit a full or absolute presence must be seen as an attempt to reduce, exclude or overcome this originary state of mediation (p. 71/104). On the other, however, the trace is what ensures that no metaphysical system can ever be complete: every attempt to establish a fully present ground or foundation will always involve a surreptitious appeal to something that, strictly speaking, is not present in order to make it good. In what is now a famous argumentative move, Derrida contends that the originary trace thus places every metaphysics of presence in a curious double-bind: it is both what makes the desire for presence *possible* in the first place and what makes the fulfilment of that desire *impossible*.

Why the 'Originary Trace'?

Why, to ask one last question, does Derrida choose to call something that is by his own admission prior to every name, concept or logic 'the originary trace'? It seems odd that he should give a name at all to something that, strictly speaking, must be unnameable! As we saw with the case of 'writing', however, his reasons for choosing this name are largely strategic: we cannot invent a new, supposedly non-metaphysical language, so it is a question of borrowing 'under erasure' the old one and turning it to our own purposes. To put it in Derrida's own words, the concept of an 'originary trace' 'destroys' the metaphysical schema that insists that every trace is the trace *of* some present being or entity (p. 61/90). Just as the idea of an *arche*-writing forces us to question exactly what we mean by a ground or founda-tion, so the concept of an originary trace can only begin to make sense if we leave behind the idea of an origin as something full, simple and singular. Once again, it is interesting to note that Derrida relates his own choice to contemporary developments within the philosoph-ical scene: Nietzsche, Heidegger, Freud and, particularly, the philoso-pher of ethics Emmanuel Levinas, are all cited as examples of thinkers who anticipate his concept of a 'trace' that can never be referred back to some moment of pure and simple presence.[12] Yet, at the same time, it is obvious that 'the trace' cannot be the 'proper name' for what Derrida is talking about in this chapter, in the sense that it offers an exclusive means of access to it that is not available to any other. If any sign only acquires its meaning from its relation to *other* signs in the system, as Derrida consistently argues, then it would obviously be wrong to suggest that only *one* sign is needed to concep-tualise this entire process. For Derrida, in other words, we cannot see the 'originary trace' as a kind of proper name or master-concept that explains all his work because it is just as subject to the process of difference, deferral and tracing it describes as any other sign. The 'originary trace' is itself dependent upon the originary trace! This is why Derrida never proposes a single or proper name for his philosophy but rather adopts a whole string of strategic 'nick-names'(usually drawn from the texts he is writing about) for the essen-tially unnameable state of mediation he is attempting to articulate: the 'trace', '*arche*-writing', '*différance*', even 'deconstruction' itself. In this sense, Derrida's own writing practice perfectly exemplifies the philosophy of language he is writing about: both are constantly shift-ing, transforming, differing/ deferring.

Conclusion

What, to go back to the question with which we began this section, might a new 'grammatology' look like? It is now becoming clear that, for Derrida, what we call 'writing' is the condition not simply of lan-guage but of any reference to the world *beyond* language too. As we will see in more detail later on, Derrida's radical claim will be that our relation to the world outside of language, whether it be to our own thoughts or to other people or things, is constantly mediated through what he calls *arche*-writing, the originary trace or *différance*: we have no pure, unmediated experience of the real. To put it somewhat dra-matically, then, Derrida's 'grammatology' is not so much the science of writing as the science of *everything*: language, consciousness, per-ception, experience and knowledge all fall within its frame of refer-ence. Yet, as Derrida goes on to show in the final chapter of Part I, which is entitled 'Of Grammatology as a Positive Science', the science of 'grammatology' also forces us to consider exactly what we *understand* by 'science' itself. If the evolution of writing is what makes all scientific knowledge possible in the first place, as we saw at the beginning of this section, then it follows that it cannot *itself* be a know-able object (p. 57/83). Perhaps more radically, however, what Derrida calls *arche*-writing – the matrix of difference, mediation and relation in which all presence is enmeshed – puts into question the very possi-bility of science itself. The classical notion of science – its projects, concepts and norms – are all fundamentally and systematically tied to the metaphysics of presence (*Positions*, p. 13). This means that the generalised writing described throughout this chapter can never be the 'object of a science', a positive entity, object or substance to be analysed, because it is the very thing that cannot let itself be reduced to 'the form of *presence*' (p. 57/83). This is why Derrida himself is so reluctant to describe his own work as a 'defence and illustration' of grammatology (*Positions*, p. 12). For Derrida, *Of Grammatology* is less about establishing a new and more rigorous science of writing so much as exploring something that risks 'destroying' [*d'ébranler*] the concept of scientific knowledge itself (p. 74/109). In Part II of the *Grammatology*, we will see how Derrida pursues this argument through an analysis of the history of writing from Rousseau to Lévi-Strauss.

Lévi-Strauss and the Violence of the Letter

In the introduction to the second part of the *Grammatology* – 'Nature, Culture, Writing' (pp. 97–100) – Derrida announces that he is now going to offer a series of historical examples to support his theoretical argument. It is important not to take this apparent shift from 'theory' into 'practice' too literally. As we have seen in the previous chapters, deconstruction teaches us to be suspicious of exactly this kind of binary thinking even if it acknowledges that we have no alternative but to continue using it. However, it *is* possible to detect a gradual shift in the trajectory of the *Grammatology* from this point onwards. To be sure, Derrida's work does not fall into any easy categories, but it is true to say that the second half of the *Grammatology* largely consists of a series of close analyses of one key figure in the history of logocentrism: the great eighteenth-century French philosopher, Jean-Jacques Rousseau. For Derrida, as we will see, it is apparently Rousseau – more than any other figure – who exemplifies everything that he has been theorising under such concepts as *arche*-writing, the originary trace and *différance*. Why, then, does Derrida accord such a pivotal status to Rousseau? How does his philosophy offer us a privileged insight into the logo-centric attempt to repress what it sees as the 'violence' of writing? To what extent, more generally, might we still be living in what Derrida calls the 'age' of Rousseau?

The Age of Rousseau

First, Derrida explicitly poses the question that will have been on the lips of his readers from the very first mention of the eighteenth-century philosopher in the *Grammatology*: why speak of Rousseau at all? It seems odd to accord such a central place to one figure within a metaphysical tradition that, as we have seen, begins with Plato and does not quite come to an end with Heidegger. According to Derrida himself, the decision is – like all his decisions – strategic and provisional rather than absolute: he is less interested in seeing 'Rousseau' as the name of a historical individual or even a body of ideas so much as a privileged *symptom* of the larger problematic of logocentrism itself (p. 99/147–8). To start with, however, Derrida does supply one very important reason for his decision: Rousseau is the only philosopher to explicitly build a *system* upon the repression of writing that generally remains implicit within the metaphysical tradition (p. 98/147). If he undoubtedly repeats the oppositional logic that is the defining gesture of the metaphysics of presence, the eighteenth-century philosopher begins from a new idea of presence itself, namely, auto-affection: the presence of the subject to itself in its own acts of consciousness or feeling. For Rousseau, as we will see in the following section, the guarantor of auto-affection is the *voice*: it is in the act of speaking, and hearing ourselves speak, that we confirm our own presence to ourselves. In Derrida's account, it is this valorisation of speech as the privileged medium of the self-present, feeling subject that motivates Rousseau's repression of the written word: writing is deemed to be a secondary extension of, or *supplement*, to the living presence of speech.

   To Derrida's way of thinking, as we will see, it is even possible to speak of an 'age' of Rousseau, such is the importance of the eighteenth-century thinker to his argument. It is a little surprising, then, that after this dramatic claim the next chapter of the *Grammatology* jumps almost 200 years forward in time to the mid-twentieth century: the chapter entitled 'The Violence of the Letter' is a detailed reading of the work of the structuralist anthropologist Claude Lévi-Strauss. At face value, Lévi-Strauss's anthropology, which is heavily influenced by Marx, Freud and, particularly, Saussure, has nothing in common with eighteenth-century philosophy. However, what interests Derrida is the extent to which even contemporary discourse is still shaped by Rousseauean ideas about speech, nature and so on and, in this respect, Lévi-Strauss is a perfect example. First of all, Derrida observes that Lévi-Strauss himself sees Rousseau as the founding father of modern anthropology: the latter was the first thinker to articulate systematically the passage from nature to culture that marks the birth of man (p. 105/154). Not only did Rousseau invent the discipline in which Lévi-Strauss works, but Lévi-Strauss also sees himself as advancing the particular ideology that is articulated within Rousseau's own thought. If Rousseau never advocates a simple return to a state of nature, as he is often accused of doing, he does argue that the form of society that would be best suited to human freedom is one that is poised between the original state of nature and civilised modernity: what he calls the first 'social contract' in his *Discourse on the Origin and Foundation of Inequality* (1755) is the primitive society that existed before the advent of the modern state.[13] For Lévi-Strauss, this diagnosis is entirely correct: the anthropologist even goes so far as to argue that a particular period in human history called the Neolithic corresponded to the ideal society described in the *Discourse* and, like Rousseau, he is deeply critical of what he sees as the degeneracy of modern civilisation. In this sense, Derrida notes, Lévi-Strauss's entire anthropological project might even be described as a 'militant Rousseauism' (p. 106/155).

Claude Lévi-Strauss (1908–) is a renowned social anthropologist whose work completely transformed the discipline of anthropology by applying the tools of structuralist linguistics to cultural analysis. His methodology is deeply influenced by Ferdinand de Saussure's pioneering studies in the field of linguistics. As we saw in the previous chapter, Saussure argued that linguists must focus on the deep-lying structures that govern language as a whole (*la langue*) as opposed to particular examples or embodiments of language (*la parole*): what makes language meaningful, Saussure contends, is the relation *between* the different elements in the system as opposed to anything intrinsic within the elements themselves. To quickly summarise his working method, Lévi-Strauss attempts to apply structuralist linguistics to the field of anthropology: culture (sexual taboos, kinship laws, marriage rites, religious rituals, social hierarchies) can be analysed in the same way as language. If previous forms of anthropology analyse particular cultural phenomena in isolation from one another, Lévi-Strauss seeks to articulate the unconscious *structures* which give those phenomena their meanings. Just as Saussure argues that linguistic terms acquire their meaning through their difference from other terms in the system, so Lévi-Strauss contends that every specific cultural phenomenon only achieves meaning within a larger network of relations and oppositions: the raw versus the cooked, the human versus the animal, the living versus the dead. In his best-selling memoir-cum-polemic, *Tristes tropiques* (literally 'sad tropics') (1955), Lévi-Strauss attacks the destructive impact of western civilisation upon non-western culture and mourns the disappearance of any 'primitive' or 'savage' society that remains untouched by western invasion.

In Derrida's view, however, it is also possible to detect a deeper philosophical identity between Rousseau and Lévi-Strauss that goes far beyond any conscious ideological solidarity between the two: both thinkers belong to the tradition that Derrida calls 'logocentrism'. This deeper, structural connection is, we will see, the real subject of 'The Violence of the Letter'. As Derrida goes on to show through a close forensic reading of Lévi-Strauss's *Tristes tropiques*, this relation takes a number of inter-linked forms. To start with, Lévi-Strauss's own methodology is also focused upon the importance of the *voice*: what inspires his own structuralist anthropology, he admits, is the specifically 'phonological' or sound-centred approach of structuralist linguistics (p. 102/151). Now, we have seen throughout this book that what appear to be neutral methodological decisions are generally the product of metaphysical presuppositions, and this is no less the case here. For Derrida, Lévi-Strauss's championing of the voice goes hand in hand with an equally Rousseauean animus towards writing: the advent of the written word is, as we will see, continually attacked by the anthropologist as a corrupt, inauthentic and even violent catastrophe that befalls the realm of speech. If Lévi-Strauss's anthropology is built upon an opposition between speech and writing, however, it is also possible to detect the entire architecture of metaphysical gestures, oppositions and hierarchies within his thought: the inside versus the outside, the natural versus the cultural, the pure versus the contaminated, and the peaceful versus the violent. The purpose of 'The Violence of the Letter' is once again to offer an 'immanent critique' of Lévi-Strauss's argument by articulating the inherent instabilities within the metaphysical logic he deploys (p. 105/154–5). This deconstruction of the work of Rousseau's most faithful modern disciple is, though, only the prelude to the larger task of Part II of the *Grammatology*: a re-evaluation of the philosophy of Rousseau himself.

The Battle of Proper Names

Second, then, I want to look in more detail at Derrida's reading of
Lévi-Strauss's *Tristes tropiques* and, in particular, of two key episodes
within the latter's narrative: the so-called 'battle of proper names' and
the 'writing lesson'. We can best observe what Derrida calls the structural homology between Lévi-Strauss and Rousseau from this vantage
point. Later on, we will see how Derrida identifies a number of
specifically Rousseauean features within Lévi-Strauss's narrative: his
reliance on an eighteenth-century rhetorical mode in what is an
allegedly scientific text, his depiction of the Nambikwara tribespeople
as living in an innocent pre-literate culture, and, finally, his condem-
nation of the 'violence' of writing – and of western civilisation more
generally – that threatens their peaceful way of life. To begin with,
however, Derrida is most interested in the highly Rousseauean way in
which Lévi-Strauss *narrates* this passage from nature to culture, from
peace to violence and from speech to writing in Nambikwara society:
what is apparently taking place here is the violation of a state of nature
by the arrival of an essentially foreign element into its midst. Now,
Lévi-Strauss himself portrays writing as something that arrives to
violate a place or moment of pure presence from 'outside', but what
Derrida is once again going to show is that this foreign body is already
intrinsic to language itself: we must articulate the 'originary violence
of a language which is always already a writing' (p. 106/156). For
Derrida, of course, all language – whether it be the 'speech' of the
Nambikwara or the 'writing' of Lévi-Strauss himself – is already a
species of a more originary and generalised 'writing' and this compels
him to re-think the Rousseauean mythology of a fall from a prelapsarian utopia. In Derrida's words, we are not dealing with a fall *from*
nature into culture, peace into violence or speech into writing so much
as a fall *within* nature itself, which is thus revealed to be never quite
'natural' in the first place.

In *Tristes tropiques*, Lévi-Strauss tells the story of a series of encounters he had with a South American tribe called the Nambikwara.
As he explains, his work was initially complicated by the fact that
the tribe were forbidden to disclose their proper names to him but,
by means of a deceit, he manages to discover the identities of the

entire group. One day, he is playing with a group of children and witnesses a little girl being struck by one of her playmates. The little girl runs up to him and whispers a 'great secret' in his ear that he does not understand. Later on, the little girl's attacker also comes up to Lévi-Strauss and, in turn, discloses another 'secret' to him.

To cut to the point of the story, Lévi-Strauss eventually gets to the bottom of what is going on between the two girls: the first little girl was trying to tell him her attacker's name and, in retaliation, the attacker decided to reveal her victim's name as well. It is thus a simple matter for him to play off all the children against one another in the same way, so that he eventually learns all their names, as well as those of the adults. However, the adults discover what the children are doing, and reprimand them for disclosing their names to the outsider. In this way, Lévi-Strauss's plot is foiled and the Nambikwara's taboo against disclosing proper names is re-established.

For Lévi-Strauss, it seems that this story is not simply an anecdote but a kind of allegory or parable about the vulnerability of the primitive utopia in which the Nambikwara live to invasion by 'civilised' western culture. It seems that the Nambikwara are attempting to protect the purity of their culture from the gaze of an outsider but this integrity is now compromised by the revelation of proper names. If anyone bears responsibility for this situation, it is the anthropologist himself: this whole scene would not have taken place, Lévi-Strauss believes, if an outsider like himself had not entered the community in bad faith and used a ruse or game to elicit the proper names of the tribe. In other words, Lévi-Strauss finds himself guilty of corrupting the very innocence he is seeking to document.

Confessions of an Anthropologist

It seems, at face value, as if Lévi-Strauss is merely recounting his own personal experience of the 'battle of proper names' but in fact this story is part of a recognisable literary genre that dates back at least as far as Rousseau's own *Social Contract*. As Derrida argues, what seems like an innocent anecdote actually belongs to an eighteenth-century tradition of confessional writing whereby autobiography is the basis for a philosophical reflection upon the relation between nature and society, between an 'ideal' society and 'real' society or, to put it more bluntly, between 'us' and 'them' (pp. 113–14/166). On the one hand, for instance, the Nambikwara people are depicted as the index of the original and natural goodness of human life: Lévi-Strauss constantly stresses their natural innocence, tenderness, sympathy and so on. On the other, however, the Nambikwara are also the sign of how far humanity has fallen since that original state: Lévi-Strauss equally confesses his own bad faith, guilt and culpability as a modern 'civilised' man throughout his dealings with the tribe. For Derrida, the larger Rousseauean agenda of this narrative is also clear: Lévi-Strauss is not so much seeking to discover the way of life of any particular people but the ideal basis of human society as a whole (p. 115/169–70). In fact, Lévi-Strauss's anthropology might be suspected of a kind of reverse ethnocentrism: what begins as an almost Marxian critique of attempts to impose western culture on other peoples as if it were a universal standard ends up setting up a thoroughly romanticised version of *non*-western culture as the ideal by which all humanity is to be judged.

The Outside and the Inside
As we have seen, then, Lévi-Strauss portrays the Nambikwara as naturally innocent, even good, in contrast to their guilty or culpable anthropologist. It is important to recognise here that this depiction of the tribe is basically just an empirical impression (based on little more than a few visits by someone who is an outsider) but what interests Derrida is how quickly Lévi-Strauss turns it into a much firmer anthropological claim. Quite simply, Lévi-Strauss is not saying 'I personally found the Nambikwara to be good people' but rather 'Nambikwara people just *are* good'. Now, what justifies this sweeping idealisation of an entire people, on the evidence of little more than a few encounters? For Derrida, it is only possible to understand this leap from the empirical to the theoretical by appreciating its *strategic* value within the overall argument of *Tristes tropiques*. What is clear is that Lévi-Strauss needs to posit the Nambikwara as an essentially pure and innocent community so that he can all the more forcefully criticise the corruption that writing visits upon them. If

Nambikwara society were not absolutely innocent, in other words, it would not be plausible for Lévi-Strauss to argue that the violence of writing and literate western culture only ever enters that society from outside: 'only such a community can suffer, as the surprise of an aggression coming *from without*, the insinuation of writing' (p. 119/174). The alternative line of argument – that writing may actually arise from within the internal structure of Nambikwara society itself – is not, apparently something that the modern follower of Rousseau is willing to contemplate. This, latter, more disturbing proposition is what Derrida's own re-reading of the 'battle of proper names' will seek to explore. In what follows, Derrida is going to argue that Lévi-Strauss's depiction of Nambikwara society as ideal, peaceful and harmonious is only possible because he has excluded something that is inherent to the make-up of that society: *arche-* or originary writing.

Originary Violence

To get to the heart of what is taking place here, Derrida goes on to explore the precise relation between writing and violence in Lévi-Strauss's account. According to Lévi-Strauss, as we will see later on, writing is inextricably linked to the exploitation of man by man: the evolution of literate culture ushers in an entirely new epoch in the history of humanity, the anthropologist argues, where power becomes concentrated in political, economic and administrative elites. Yet, because the Nambikwara still belong within a pre-literate culture, he believes that they have, until now, been largely immune to the kind of power politics that characterises modern western civilisation. Unfortunately, Lévi-Strauss's *own* personal experiences of the Nambikwara often fly in the face of this attempt to portray them as an essentially peaceable, non-violent people: the anthropologist recounts numerous incidents of violence, conflict and inequality in tribal life.[14] For Derrida, in other words, it is clear that – contrary to Lévi-Strauss's declarations – this supposedly pre-literate, primitive utopia is actually riven with violence and this compels him to look in more detail at what is really going on in the battle of proper names. Now, Derrida accepts Lévi-Strauss's argument that there is an essential relation between writing and violence – writing mediates, interrupts or compromises what should be a pure and undifferentiated state of presence – but he is going to argue that this takes place at a deeper, more structural, level than has previously been supposed. In Derrida's account, the 'violence of the letter' is not something that befalls the Nambikwara from without but, as we have already begun to suggest, rather something that is intrinsic to the structure of that tribal society itself: violence is originary.

The Three Levels of Violence

In Derrida's view, it is actually possible to tease out three different levels of violence that are collapsed together within Lévi-Strauss's account of the battle of proper names. It is too simplistic, in other words, to see the story of the disclosure of the proper names as the passage from peace to violence, as the anthropologist does, because in fact an originary state of 'peace' has never existed in the first place. As he re-reads Lévi-Strauss's own account (pp. 111–12/164–6), Derrida delineates a very complex tripartite structure of violence that is interwoven all the way through Nambikwara society:

1. First of all, Derrida argues that the very institution of proper names within Nambikwara society is *itself* an act of violence: to name is already to violate. It is important to grasp straightaway that Derrida is articulating a concept of 'violence' here that takes place on a much more general or abstract level than the empirical act of force that Lévi-Strauss is talking about, but its effect is the same. According to Saussure's differential theory of language – which, as we have seen, heavily influences Lévi-Strauss's anthropology – a proper name can only *be* proper if it exists in a relation to other proper names: 'Peter' is only meaningful because it is different from 'Mary'. Now, the upshot of this position is that no name can ever be 'proper' in and of itself – in the sense that it refers solely, directly and uniquely, to what it names – and this leads Derrida to speak of the 'death' of absolutely proper naming (p. 109/164). To Derrida's eyes, in other words, it thus becomes possible to speak of an 'originary' violence at work in the act of naming because the very structure of language itself *violates* the supposed propriety, the supposedly unique status, of the proper name: 'Anterior to the possibility of violence in the current and derivative sense' he argues, we find 'the violence of the *arche*-writing, the violence of difference, of classification, and of

the system of appellations' (p. 110/162). For Derrida, we can thus detect an essential relation between writing and violence even within the supposedly pre-literate, peaceful culture of the Nambikwara: what Lévi-Strauss calls proper names have *already* been expropriated – violated, compromised, contaminated – by the very fact of their inscription within the system of linguistic difference, relation and mediation that Derrida names *arche*-writing. In other words, the violation of proper names has already been perpetrated by language before Lévi-Strauss even arrives on the scene and uses trickery to elicit their disclosure.

2. After the violent institution of 'proper' names, though, comes a second violence: the Nambikwara's attempt to censor or prohibit the disclosure of those names to Lévi-Strauss. To put it in a word, then, Derrida argues that the second level of violence is the institution of *law*. However, once again this seems a somewhat strange move to make: law is commonly seen as that which puts an end to violence, that which restores or protects a state of peace, so why see it as representing a new form of violence? Quite simply, the answer is that what we call the 'law' can only meet violence *with* violence. The institution of law by the Nambikwara cannot actually restore an original state of peace in which all proper names are respected, for no such state ever existed, so all it can do is more or less violently suppress the violence of language itself under the guise of 'justice' 'morality' or 'society'. This apparent attempt to preserve the so-called 'proper' names by forbidding their disclosure is, Derrida argues, thus actually what makes those names proper in the first place. For Derrida, then, it is the identification of, and prohibition against, something called 'impropriety' that produces the illusion of a pre-existing state of 'propriety'. In other words, the institution of law manufactures the very state of original 'propriety' it claims to protect: 'the so-called proper, substitute of the deferred proper, *perceived* by the *social* and *moral consciousness* as the proper' (p. 112/165).

3. Finally, though, there is also a third level of violence going on in this little scene: the physical act of breaking or transgressing the law that takes place when Lévi-Strauss tricks the girls into disclosing their names to him. It is only now that Derrida's analysis arrives at something close to what is commonly understood by the term 'violence',

namely, a physical or empirical force that is illegitimately exerted by one party upon another. Yet, even here, things are not quite as simple as they might seem. For Derrida, this third kind of violence may or may not actually take place in empirical reality – whether Lévi-Strauss decides to trick the girls into disclosing their names is, of course, entirely up to him – but it is *always* a possibility because it is the logical outworking of the violence inherent in its two predecessors. What makes possible the empirical violence wrought against the proper name by the anthropologist, in other words, is the *impossibility* of the proper name ever establishing itself either linguistically or by the institution of law. In this sense, Lévi-Strauss's own act of illegality does not so much *break* the law as *expose* the violence inherent in what is called 'law' (p. 112/165).

What, then, is the real significance of the battle of proper names? For Derrida, this story reveals that the violence *of* writing – the network of differences, relations and mediation which interrupts every pure, unique or self-identical meaning – is at work within Nambikwara society long before the advent of writing in the accepted, empirical sense of that term: what Lévi-Strauss persists in calling 'peace' is already a state of violence. In the next part of the chapter, Derrida pursues this insight into a reading of another pivotal scene in *Tristes tropiques* called the 'writing lesson'.

The Writing Lesson
Finally, then, I want to move on to the most important site of Derrida's engagement with Lévi-Strauss's anthropology: the scene in *Tristes tropiques* where the anthropologist apparently teaches the Nambikwara how to write. It is in his account of the 'writing lesson' that Lévi-Strauss offers his most rigorous and systematic analysis of the historical meaning of writing. All the same, everything within this account confirms the Rousseauean agenda that we have already begun to see in the battle of proper names: the adoption of an eighteenth-century confessional mode, the idealisation of Nambikwara culture as essentially innocent and, of course, the corruption of that innocence through the sudden arrival of modernity in the form of writing. To Derrida's eyes, it is once again crucial to note how this passage from a prelapsarian utopia to the fallen world of modernity is depicted:

what takes place is again presented as a violation of a prelapsarian utopia from outside because it is none other than *Lévi-Strauss himself* who teaches the Nambikwara to write. If Lévi-Strauss again tries to show how the arrival of writing corrupts what was a hitherto innocent society – because it marks the beginning of the kind of exploitation that characterises western 'civilisation' – Derrida will once again be concerned to demonstrate the exact opposite: a deeper and more essential *arche*-writing is already at work within Nambikwara society itself before empirical writing ever appears on the scene. For Derrida, in other words, an 'originary' writing appears well before writing in the narrow sense: it is 'already in the *différance* or the *arche*-writing that opens speech itself' (p. 128/186). In this sense, what Lévi-Strauss calls the 'writing lesson' has always already been learnt by the Nambikwara.

In *Tristes tropiques*, Lévi-Strauss tells the story of another 'extraordinary incident' in his life with the Nambikwara. To begin with, Lévi-Strauss describes how he once distributed pencils and sheets of paper to the small Nambikwara group he was staying with in order to see what they did with them. According to Lévi-Strauss, the Nambikwara belong to a purely oral culture: they may draw decorative patterns on the shells of their gourds but they do not know what writing is. However, armed with their new tools, the tribespeople instantly began to scribble wavy, horizontal lines on the pads he has given them. If this development surprises him, given their total ignorance of written language, the anthropologist has a simple explanation: the Nambikwara are merely imitating, in a child-like way, his own act of writing and drawing without really understanding what they are doing. For Lévi-Strauss, the only member of the tribe who seems to come close to grasping the true purpose of writing is the chief: he not only scribbles horizontal lines on his pad in imitation of the anthropologist but pretends that these lines possess a meaning, which he then goes on to 'read' out to the group.

Then Lévi-Strauss moves on to recount another encounter with the Nambikwara that casts their 'writing lesson' in a new, and more disturbing, light. After the first incident, he asks the tribal chief to take him to visit other Nambikwara groups so that he can begin to build up a more complete anthropological profile of the tribe as a whole. However, the visiting party are met with obvious hostility by the other tribal group. To appease his angry hosts, the chief says that the two groups should exchange gifts. Now, this is a familiar tribal ritual, but Lévi-Strauss recounts how the chief introduces an entirely new element into the procedure: he takes out his writing pad and begins to 'read' out the list of gifts that are to be exchanged between the two groups. For Lévi-Strauss, this almost farcical charade is strangely irritating to watch but it is only later that he is able to put his finger on what is troubling him: the tribal chief has, the anthropologist thinks, intuitively grasped something disturbing about the nature of writing itself. The chief has 'borrowed' the tool of writing not in order to attain greater understanding, for he has obviously not learnt how to write in such a short period of time, but to falsely enhance his own prestige and authority at the expense of the rest of the party. This pre-literate tribesman has realised that writing is not simply an instrument for knowledge, in other words, but a means of attaining and wielding *power*.

Finally, Lévi-Strauss goes on to draw a number of large world-historical conclusions about the nature, status and purpose of writing from his encounter with the Nambikwara chief. To start with, he argues that writing has always been the privileged tool of a powerful elite as opposed to a mere instrument for extending knowledge, understanding or communication: the written word is, he says, the medium of man's exploitation by man. It is customary for anthropologists to identify the invention of alphabetic writing at around 4000 BCE with a massive transformation in human culture, society and civilisation. However, Lévi-Strauss argues that there are good reasons for questioning the apparent link between the invention of writing and the growth of knowledge. On the one hand, for example, the Neolithic period predates the appearance of any known system of writing but it is still commonly agreed to have been a period of huge advancements in culture, knowledge and so on. On the other, the period from the invention of writing up until the scientific revolutions of the nineteenth century was marked by a comparative intellectual stagnation: the quantity of knowledge, he says, did not markedly increase in that period. If the epoch of writing is characterised by anything, it is less the advancement of knowledge than the extension of power, domination and segregation through political, economic and administrative elites: the historic function of writing has been to reinforce the power of the few rather than to bring knowledge to the many. For Lévi-Strauss, this process continues apace as western culture, knowledge and languages become increasingly globalised: what is presented as a tool of social, economic and intellectual empowerment for the rest of the world actually represents another means of control, power and exploitation. In the simple act of teaching the Nambikwara how to write, Lévi-Strauss himself has unwittingly contributed to the corruption of a pure and innocent state of nature by introducing power, violence and manipulation into its midst.

The Extraordinary Incident

It is revealing, once again, that Derrida begins his analysis of the 'writing lesson' with a critique of the *genre* in which Lévi-Strauss has chosen to couch his observations. Of course, Derrida finds Lévi-Strauss's story beautifully constructed but it is this very artfulness that leads him to suspect that something more complex than just personal or empirical observation is going on here. What is being narrated here is no mere anecdote but another Rousseauean parable about the corruption of a state of nature by the arrival of society. For Derrida, it is crucial to note this constant and uncritical traffic from autobiography to anthropology, empiricism to theory, fact to interpretation that goes on in *Tristes tropiques* because it is here that the larger assumptions guiding his narrative reveal themselves (p. 126/184). If Lévi-Strauss constantly bends, or even ignores, the evidence of his own testimony in order to suit his larger theoretical strategy, this strategy is not merely evidence of his complicity with a Rousseauist mythology of origins but with the larger tradition of logocentrism that is the target of the *Grammatology*. In Derrida's own words, Lévi-Strauss's 'writing lesson' is the 'finest example of the metaphysics of presence' (p. 131/191).

The People without Writing?
To start with, Derrida again concentrates on probing Lévi-Strauss's personal account of the 'extraordinary incident' of the writing lesson. It goes without saying that the whole premise of the writing lesson is that the Nambikwara have no prior knowledge whatsoever of writing – why would Lévi-Strauss need to teach them if they did? – but it is just this presumption that Derrida seeks to question. As he goes on to show, it is possible to challenge Lévi-Strauss's reasons for believing the Nambikwara to be a 'people without writing' on a number of grounds:

1. First, Derrida considers Lévi-Strauss's claim that the Nambikwara must be a pre-literate people because they have no word in their language for 'writing': the closest equivalent is 'iekariukedjutu' which means 'drawing lines'. If this fact may well be true, it is something of a leap to say that it tells us anything about Nambikwara culture in general. Is the fact that they do not have an exactly equivalent *word* for 'writing' evidence that they do not know *how* to write?

2. The Nambikwara do inscribe patterns on the shells of their gourds, of course, but Lévi-Strauss says these do not qualify as writing in the strict sense because they have a purely decorative or 'aesthetic' function. Here, too, though, Derrida finds problems. Is it appropriate to use a western classical concept like 'aesthetics' in this very different context? More generally, is it possible to simply isolate the *aesthetic* function of writing from its *utilitarian* function as if one were more integral than the other?

3. This problem is compounded later on in *Tristes tropiques* when Lévi-Strauss recounts how the Nambikwara also use writing not simply for aesthetic purposes but for genealogical ones (p. 125/182–4). On one level, this is not surprising: the desire to record and conserve family trees in a more enduring form than human memory or speech is generally agreed to be the main impetus behind the emergence of empirical writing. For Derrida, however, what is of interest here is the complex systems of genealogical classification that the Nambikwara already have in place before the advent of writing in the empirical sense of the term: Lévi-Strauss is staggered, for instance, by the ability of the tribespeople to recite family trees that stretch back dozens of generations. What is clear is that the Nambikwara already

possess the kind of systematic network of differences, relations and mediations that characterise 'writing' in the general sense of the term even if they do not necessarily inscribe that network in empirical form. Why, then is Lévi-Strauss so insistent that the Nambikwara are an oral, pre-literate people who are only now learning how to write? Could we not say that what is taking place here is less a passage from *speech* to writing and more a passage from one form of *writing* to another? To what extent might we see this kind of complex genealogical taxonomy – with different classes, relations and lineages – as evidence of what Derrida calls '*arche*-writing'?

In summary, then, Derrida is once again interested in moving beyond Lévi-Strauss's narrow and empirical concept of writing in order to articulate a more essential or originary writing that is at work even with Nambikwara culture itself: what is supposedly an oral, pre-literate culture already exists in a relation to writing.

Man's Exploitation by Man

For Derrida, however, what is most interesting about the writing lesson is not its effect upon the Nambikwara, but the series of vast, world-historical lessons about writing that Lévi-Strauss himself professes to learn from it (p. 126/184). We have already seen that it is the Nambikwara chief's appropriation of writing in order to obtain greater power and prestige that leads Lévi-Strauss to the conclusion that the story of writing is nothing less than the story of man's exploitation by man. Once again, however, Derrida professes his shock at how weakly empirical Lévi-Strauss's argument is here: what is little more than an anecdote about one tribal group becomes the basis for a series of enormous speculations about the history of human civilisation (p. 126/184). To put it somewhat bluntly, Lévi-Strauss's theory is so vast, so full of questionable assumptions and sweeping statements that it is neither verifiable nor falsifiable (p. 129/188):

1. First, Derrida questions the founding assumption on which Lévi-Strauss's rests: the invention of writing and scientific and cultural progress have little or nothing to do with one another. It is only by cleaving the practice of writing from the pursuit of knowledge in this

way that Lévi-Strauss is able to advance his central thesis: the written word is principally a means for the arrogation of *power*. However, we have already seen in the last chapter that, if anything, the exact opposite is the case. For Derrida, scientific knowledge is contingent upon the invention of writing: any objective or universal truth that remains the same for everyone, everywhere throughout space and time is only possible on the basis of it being preserved, recorded and transmitted *through* writing. In fact, Lévi-Strauss's anthropological project, which seeks to offer a rigorous, scientific account of human culture, can scarcely be said to exist *outside* this history. Could it not be argued that Lévi-Strauss's own work gains its scientific credentials from the very thing that he is attacking as inimical to the advancement of knowledge?

2. Upon Lévi-Strauss's reading, however, the best proof of his theory that writing is not an essential condition of scientific progress is *historical*. To clinch his argument, he cites the example of the Neolithic period: this epoch is generally agreed to have witnessed massive and unprecedented advancements in human knowledge, culture and so on.[15] Yet, all this took place *before* the invention of alphabetic script, so writing could hardly be said to be integral to the advancement of knowledge. Now, Derrida does not dispute the singular importance of the Neolithic within the history of human culture, but what he does question is the assumption that it did not contain any system of writing. For Derrida, we can detect a somewhat narrow definition of writing at work in Lévi-Strauss's account that leads him to ignore the long history of systems of inscribing and archiving information that *preceded* the appearance of the alphabet around 4000 BCE: why do they not merit the name of 'writing'? If Derrida casts doubt on the idea that Neolithic culture was pre-literate, he also calls into question Lévi-Strauss's totally unverifiable claim that the 'quantity' of knowledge has remained largely the same in the period since the invention of alphabetic writing (p. 129/188–9). What exactly is a 'quantity' of knowledge anyway? Can we measure or count knowledge like beans? Is not the concept of 'quantity' – of number, of calculus, of mathematics – *itself part of* the sum of modern knowledge that is supposedly being quantified here?

3. In Lévi-Strauss's account, of course, all these attempts to argue that the invention of writing is not principally a tool for knowledge are

merely the flip side of his real claim: writing *is* the instrument of man's exploitation of man. Derrida agrees that this claim may well be historically incontestable: the invention of writing undoubtedly makes possible both the concentration of power in the hands of a small elite and the delegation, deferment or stockpiling of power. Arguably, Lévi-Strauss has not gone far enough in asserting the relation between writing and power: Derrida would say that even the most primitive agricultural societies begin to possess a kind of *arche*-writing from the moment they begin to organise themselves in a economic way by deferring immediate consumption of their harvests, putting produce into reserve for the next season and so on (p. 130/190). Moreover, Derrida questions what he sees as an uncritical tendency in Lévi-Strauss's work to simply equate the establishment of political hierarchies with political exploitation and domination: '[p]olitical power [for Lévi-Strauss – AB] can only be the custodian of an unjust power' (p. 131/191). For Derrida, it is possible to detect a latent anarchism in Lévi-Strauss's suspicion of *all* forms of social organisation as agents of oppression, enslavement and subordination. If Derrida does not necessarily disagree with this hypothesis – he goes out of his way to say that it is a credible one – what bothers him is that once again it is nothing *more* than a hypothesis: Lévi-Strauss simply seems to assume that the 'violence' of modern civilisation is every bit as self-evident as the 'peacefulness' of ancient, pre-literate cultures.[16] What, again, is the historical or rational basis for this claim? Can we simply equate law with enslavement? Might we not just as easily argue that the institution of law guarantees or extends *liberty*?

For Derrida, then, it is clear that something much more complicated than a simple narrative of decline and fall is taking place in Lévi-Strauss's history of writing: whatever values the anthropologist present in black and white terms – nature versus culture, speech versus writing, peace versus violence – end up merging imperceptibly into one another. Why, then, does Lévi-Strauss persist in believing that the appearance of writing is a catastrophe that befalls the state of nature?

The Age of Rousseau

In Derrida's view, the answer to this question is obvious: Lévi-Strauss's anthropological discourse is entirely shaped by a Rousseauean mythology of origins. We might say that the Nambikwara are merely a modern version of the Romantic 'natural man' or 'noble savage'. This mythology of a 'speech originally good, and of a violence which would come to pounce upon it as a fatal accident' (p. 135/195) is the backdrop for Lévi-Strauss's powerful critique of writing. As we saw with Saussure's linguistic theory in the previous chapter, however, structuralist anthropology is, for all its scientific pretensions, an accomplice to the speculative dogmatism that is logocentrism. To put it simply, Lévi-Strauss's attempt to valorise Nambikwara life over and against modern civilisation merely reproduces what we have seen to be the classic metaphysical hierarchies of presence over absence, speech over writing and so on: this oral, immediate, self-present community – 'a community of speech where all members are within earshot' (p. 135/195) – exists outside of the violent, inauthentic, written world of history. Yet, once again, Derrida has shown through a careful re-reading of *Tristes tropiques* that this oppositional logic does not stand up. Everything that Lévi-Strauss tries to place *outside* Nambikwara life (writing, violence, culture) can be found at work *inside* it. If Derrida's strategy will already be familiar to us from his readings of Husserl, Saussure *et al.*, it remains the case that there is a particularly poignant irony in his deconstruction of Lévi Strauss's anthropological project: what the anthropologist presents as a critique of western values – a humane, anti-colonial, progressive ethnology (p. 120/175–6) – is itself the product of the definingly western tradition of logocentrism. For Derrida, we might say that the true moral of the 'writing lesson' is once again the impossibility of ever simply resisting or escaping the metaphysics of presence.

Conclusion
What, then, is Derrida's larger purpose in this critique of Lévi-Strauss? It is clear that Lévi-Strauss uncovers an important and hitherto unrecognised relation between writing and violence in his work on the Nambikwara, but this relation goes much deeper than the neo-Rousseauean anthropologist himself supposes. As Derrida writes, what Lévi-Strauss calls the violence of writing is nothing less than the original condition of language itself: we are already disturbed, expropriated, violated from the moment we begin to speak. To be sure,

Derrida's attempt to posit an originary violence within the primitivist utopia occupied by the Nambikwara is not to deny the violence that western colonialism has wreaked upon them, nor to imply a moral equivalence between coloniser and colonised, but it *is* a way of calling into question the possibility of any pure or absolute moral good: whatever we call 'peace', however desirable or justifiable it may be, *always* contains the traces of violence. If he is often accused of being an ethical relativist or nihilist, the philosopher actually sees the concept of the originary violence of writing as the basis for a new ethics. For Derrida, as we will see in the conclusion of this book, the originary state of mediation that he calls *différance*, *arche*-writing, the originary trace – where the 'other' is continually announced within the 'same' as its condition of possibility – appears to have an inescapably ethical dimension: 'There is no ethics without the presence of the other but also, and consequently, without absence, disimulation, detour, *différance*, writing' (p. 140/202). In the next section, however, we will see how Derrida turns his attention from Lévi-Strauss to the main target of Part II of the *Grammatology*: Jean-Jacques Rousseau himself.

Rousseau: The Logic of the Supplement

For Derrida, it is now clear what the main task of Part II of the *Grammatology* must be: a reading of the philosophy of Jean-Jacques Rousseau. As we have already hinted on a number of occasions, it is with Rousseau, that all the ideas he has been articulating throughout the text – the metaphysics of presence, logocentrism, the repression and subsequent return of something called *arche*-writing – find their most concrete expression. Quite simply, then, it is impossible to exaggerate the significance of the eighteenth-century philosopher for Derrida's overall argument. To put it in his own words, Derrida does not see 'Rousseau' as just one more name in the long history of metaphysics so much as the name of an entire epoch: 'what may perhaps be called the "age" of Rousseau' (p. lxxxix/7). If there are many reasons why Derrida chooses to stake so much on one figure, the most important one is that the philosopher is apparently the only thinker within the modern epoch to build an explicit theme or system upon the repression of writing: Rousseau champions an organic

co............................n word as the kind of society best
sui...........................cks the advent of writing as the
beg..........................ity and corruption that charac-
teri.........................then, is Derrida's response to
Ro...........................his apparent opposition between
speech and writing, nature and culture, freedom and enslavement? To
what extent might we find an *arche*-writing at work between and
within this set of oppositions? In what follows, Derrida will seek to
show how what Rousseau calls the 'dangerous supplement' to speech,
presence and nature – writing – is in fact the originary *condition* of the
state of nature.

The Supplement

First, Derrida offers an introduction to his reading of Rousseau in the
brief chapter entitled '. . . That Dangerous Supplement . . . [*Ce
dangereux supplément*]'. It will be very clear by now that what follows will
not be an external critique of Rousseau so much as a 'deconstruction'
of the logic that is operative in his texts. As with the cases of Saussure,
Lévi-Strauss *et al.*, Derrida will oppose Rousseau to no one but
Rousseau himself: the philosopher who condemns writing as a
dangerous force that corrupts speech is also, we will see, the philosopher who consistently resorts to writing as a corrective to, or protec-
tive against, the deficiencies of speech. For Derrida, Rousseau's
philosophy is of interest not because it depicts a fall from an essentially oral state of nature into the iniquities of modern civil society,
as many believe, but rather because once again it reveals a kind
of internal crisis *within* nature itself: the great critic of writing is
also deeply sceptical of the illusion of full and present speech
(p. 140/202). If 'That Dangerous Supplement' is now one of the
most famous chapters in the entire *Grammatology*, it is also – and particularly for readers new to Derrida – one of the most idiosyncratic:
Derrida's reading constantly tacks back and forth between Rousseau's
life and work and seems to treat everything from the philosopher's
most personal confessions to his largest theoretical claims as grist to
his own mill. In 'The Exorbitant: Question of Method', a brief essay
that concludes the chapter, Derrida offers a defence of this particular
way of reading and of the methodology of deconstructive reading
more generally.

Jean-Jacques Rousseau (1712–78) was one of the most important philosophers of the eighteenth century. His works number not only philosophical treatises on politics, education and the arts but auto-biography and fiction: well-known texts include *Discourse on the Origin and Foundations of Inequality* (1754), *Émile; or, on Education* (1762), *The Social Contract* (1762) and *Confessions* (1771). As he makes clear from his earliest work onwards, Rousseau's philosophy seeks to address the question of whether the current state of modern civil society is best suited to the natural needs of human beings. To Rousseau's way of thinking, human beings are essentially good when they exist in the state of nature but are gradually corrupted by the creation of civil society. Yet, in spite of this, it is important to stress that Rousseau does not believe that a return to the state of nature is either possible or desirable, even though many critics, including the great thinker of the French Enlightenment, Voltaire, attributed such a view to him. For Rousseau, it is only possible to overcome the inequality of civil society through the institution of a new form of sovereignty – the Social Contract – that is both an expression of the general will of the citizens and something that applies equally to every citizen alike. If Rousseau's theory of the goodness of man in the state of nature is the basis of his political theory, it is also the starting point of his philosophy of education: *Émile* argues that the goal of education is not to counter or domes-ticate our natural tendencies but rather to cultivate them. In many ways, Rousseau's legacy as a thinker is impossible to exaggerate: his political philosophy was championed by the leaders of the French Revolution at the end of the eighteenth century and he was an essential touchstone for Enlightenment, Romantic and modern liberal thought.

Writing and Speech

First, Derrida briefly explicates Rousseau's ambivalent attitude towards writing. It is here that many of the themes, moves and ges-tures that we have been tracing through our readings of Saussure, Lévi-Strauss *et al.* originate. As we will see in the next section, Rousseau's *Essay on the Origin of Languages* offers perhaps the defining logocentric account of the relation between speech and writing: Rousseau argues that the spoken word naturally expresses our present thoughts whereas the written word erects an unnecessary material barrier between thought and expression. For Rousseau, predictably, writing starts to become dangerous when it does not merely mediate thought but comes to *substitute* for it: what begins as merely a representation of something ends up becoming confused with the thing itself. Now, we have already seen that this is a recurring fear in the history of logocentrism: Saussure, for instance, is just as fearful of a modern, decadent, culture where the signifier is becoming confused with the signified, the representation with the real presence (p. 42/62–3). However, Rousseau's distrust of writing is not simply a matter of linguistics: it also has an irreducibly political dimension. On the one hand, the spoken word is represented as the guarantor of the kind of organic, undivided, self-present community that, for Rousseau, represents the ideal form of human organisation: a community where every member is within earshot, where every citizen must engage in face-to-face relations, is one without inequality, hierarchy or division. On the other, however, the written word represents the beginning of modern civil society with all its impersonal structures, inequalities and divisions: a community where members communicate via writing is one that is already starting to disperse, fragment or disappear (p. 138/199–200). In this sense, Rousseau argues that the story of the passage from speech to writing is inextricably tied to the larger story of humanity's decline and fall from the state of nature to the decadence of modern civil society.

Writing Supplements Speech

It is not quite this simple, however. Unfortunately, we can detect a kind of 'performative contradiction' at work in Rousseau's philosophy of writing: what he says and what he does do not always match up (p. 144/207). To be sure, Rousseau constantly attacks writing as a corruption of speech but, at the same time, he consistently represents it as a necessary corrective or supplement to a certain deficiency within speech itself. He famously claims that he has written his autobiographical *Confessions*, for instance, because the element of distance afforded by the written word will enable him to reveal his true nature much better than he could if he himself were present in the room talking to us (p. 142/204–5).[17] Yet, how can this claim about the power of writing to communicate his true nature be squared with his argument that writing is a dehumanising or denaturalising force? If the very act of writing would seem to surrender all possibility of presence – Rousseau is obviously not 'there' in person when we read the *Confessions* – it now seems that this self-sacrifice is carried out with the goal of communicating that presence all the more securely: it is actually an act of self-aggrandisement (p. 143/205–6). For Derrida, it thus becomes possible to detect a strange tension at work in Rousseau's theory that he will worry at throughout this chapter: writing is what actually gives us access to the very self-presence that is supposedly the preserve of speech alone. The spoken word is ostensibly sufficient as a medium for communicating presence but, as we will see, it requires supplementation by writing in order to complete the job. This is why the great philosopher of speech must immerse himself in the act of writing in order to ensure that his true meaning and value is not misunderstood. In Derrida's account, then, Rousseau's theory accomplishes almost the exact opposite of its apparent intention: what is revealed is less the destructive impact of writing than the fallibility of speech.

The Logic of the Supplement

To explain what is going on here, Derrida once again has recourse to an ambiguous term drawn from Rousseau's own text: the 'supplement' (*le supplément*). This key term in Rousseau's thought enables Derrida to articulate the logic of difference, relation and mediation that he elsewhere names *arche*-writing, the originary trace and *différance*. Of course, the name may be different but the effect is the same: the supplement is another way of theorising the fact that every apparently self-identical presence depends upon what it places outside, below, or after itself in order to obtain even the effect of identity. Derrida goes on to argue that figure of the supplement carries two essentially contradictory significations within Rousseau's text. On the one hand, the supplement can be an *addition* to something that is already full, present and sufficient in itself: it is a surplus that merely enriches, accumulates and preserves what is in itself 'the *fullest measure* [*le comble*]' of presence (p. 144/208). On the other, however, the *supplement* can be an essential *substitute*, or compensation for, something that is essentially lacking, insufficient, or in need of supplementation in itself: it intervenes '*in-the-place-of* . . . as if one fills a void [*s'il comble un vide*]' (p. 145/208). For Derrida, then, the supplement plays two radically different roles: it either confirms an originary presence that is complete in itself or – as we have just seen in the case of writing – it reveals an essential lack, or deficiency, of presence that calls for supplementation in the first place. If we can see both of these significations at work in Rousseau's text, what Derrida is going to argue is that these contradictory meanings are logically intertwined within one another: what *produces* the impression of any full or immediate presence is nothing less than the supplements that come to compensate for its absence. In a sense that will now be very familiar to us, there is no 'real presence': supplementation goes all the way down.

In the *Confessions* (1771), Rousseau presents what is generally agreed to be the first work of modern autobiography. His autobiography differs from all previous such works by St Augustine of Hippo and St Teresa of Avila because it is a personal, as opposed to a spiritual, account of its author's life and experiences. To put it in his own words, Rousseau tries to do something that has never before been attempted: '[m]y purpose is to display to my kind a portrait in every way true to nature, and the man I shall portray will be myself' (*Confessions*, p. 17). What follows is the story of his life from his humble upbringing in Geneva (Rousseau's mother died in childbirth and his father abandoned him) to his mature position as a philosopher of international celebrity and notoriety. The *Confessions* also provides an account of the experiences that shaped Rousseau's philosophy and, as such, it is something of a personal companion to the more theoretical meditation on education entitled *Émile: Or, On Education*. This work is also remarkable for its (at least apparent) honesty and candour: Rousseau openly recounts a number of intimate, painful and/or humiliating episodes in his life from childhood acts of deceit to his adult sex life.

Rousseau's Supplements
In the remainder of the *Grammatology*, Derrida traces what he calls this 'logic' of supplementation at work throughout Rousseau's body of

texts: the *Confessions*, the treatise on education *Émile*, and the *Essay on the Origin of Languages*. He chooses to begin this reading by looking at Rousseau's celebrated autobiography. As we saw above, the very fact that Rousseau chooses to write this autobiography in the first place is evidence of the logic of supplementation Derrida is talking about: the veil of the written word is apparently the only means by which the philosopher can reveal himself as he really is. What other examples, though, can we find of this logic in action?

1. To start with, Derrida returns to Rousseau's founding thesis that the state of nature is entirely pure and self-sufficient. Nature requires no supplement of any kind to perfect it. However, this argument raises the inevitable question of why, if the state of nature lacked nothing, civil society ever appeared in the first place: why didn't things just stay as they were? For Rousseau, just as in the case of Lévi-Strauss some 200 years later, the answer is that culture, art, science and every other supplement are an essentially unnatural force that invade nature from *outside*: 'Nature's supplement does not proceed from Nature' (*Grammatology*, p. 145/209).

2. According to Derrida, however, Rousseau's texts can supply another, more compelling, answer to the question of why nature is supplemented: it requires supplementation because it is *incomplete* in itself. For Rousseau the pure self-sufficiency of nature is typified by maternal love: there is no substitute, he says, for a mother's love (p. 145/209). To attempt to fill that state of nature with anything else – art, science, society – is to substitute an inferior, unnatural, substitute for the real thing. Unfortunately, though, this is exactly what Rousseau himself sets out to do: *Émile* proposes educational reforms in order to instil in children the qualities necessary to become responsible adults and citizens. Now there is an obvious contradiction in Rousseau's text here. What is education if not a *supplement* for the apparently irreplaceable virtues of maternal love?

3. So: Rousseau's philosophy of education is the very supplement to nature that he otherwise deems unnecessary. It may well be that there is no substitute for maternal love, but even Rousseau admits that a healthy nurse is better than a sick mother (p. 146/209–10). Indeed, there is also the question of the natural weakness of the *child* itself: the reason why education is necessary is because it cultivates the qualities

of strength, self-reliance and emotional stability that children do not naturally possess. If nature provides us with everything we need to sustain ourselves, then why does it allow children to be born so weak, indeed, why does it allow children *at all* (p. 146/210)? The state of nature is presented as self-sufficient, in other words, but it contains a lack that requires supplementation. This creates a paradoxical situation within Rousseau's thought whereby his philosophy of education comes into conflict with his political critique of civil society. In other words, the very thing that makes human *progress* possible – the supplement – is also the beginning of humanity's *fall* into the corruption of civil society (p. 147/211).

For Derrida, then, it is clear that Rousseau's attempt to establish an *opposition* between nature and the unnatural, the inside and the outside, the thing itself and the unnecessary supplement cannot control the differential logic that *binds* all these concepts together: each term cannot exist without the other. The state of nature is not a pure or complete presence that is corrupted from without by inferior or unnatural supplements, in other words, but an originary lack that stands in need of supplementation. This supplement thus does not arrive into a pure or complete nature after the fact but rather emerges from a gap at the heart of 'nature' itself. In Derrida's paradoxical terminology, then, we can begin to speak of a 'natural' supplement in the same way that we have spoken of an *arche*-writing or an 'originary' trace: 'the supplement comes naturally to put itself in Nature's place' (p. 149/214).

The Chain of Supplements

Second, though, Derrida goes on to analyse one very intimate example of this 'logic of the supplement' at work in Rousseau's text in more detail: masturbation. It is in the *Confessions*, appropriately enough, that Rousseau recounts his first experience of what he calls 'this dangerous means' (*ce dangereux supplément*) of relieving his sexual frustrations (*Confessions*, p. 108). As with the other cases, however, Derrida detects a distinct ambiguity in the philosopher's attitude towards auto-eroticism. To put it in a word, Rousseau once again sees masturbation as a *supplement* (in both senses of the word) to nature, to health and to sexual relations with women. On the one hand, masturbation is depicted as an *unnatural* vice: it corrupts the natural constitution, wastes energy and substitutes an array of fantasies for the 'real thing'. On the other, however, masturbation is also seen as an entirely *natural* act: it springs from natural desires even if its effect is to waste, abuse or destroy nature itself (p. *Grammatology*, p. 151/216). If Rousseau usually tends to depict auto-eroticism as an evil that befalls the natural integrity of the subject from outside, for example, it is also revealing that the philosopher claims sole responsibility for his own corruption: nothing is *more* natural to him, it would seem, than this corruption of nature. For Derrida, it is once again the case that masturbation is the product of a certain lack or deficiency within the state of nature that requires supplementation: nature de-naturalises itself.

The Supplement restores Presence

However, masturbation is not simply one more supplement for Rousseau, Derrida argues. On the contrary, it also tells us something about the *logic* of supplementation itself. As the *Confessions* make clear, what began as an outlet for a frustrated adolescent persists into adult-hood: indeed, Rousseau eventually abandons hetero-erotic relations with women altogether in favour of auto-eroticism. Quite simply, Derrida argues that Rousseau's masturbation begins to assume a role that is *greater* than that of a mere 'supplement' to nature: what should be an inferior substitute for a more complete and satisfying form of sexual experience actually becomes the only means of experiencing satisfaction completely and directly. If Rousseau prefers to give up sex for masturbation, Derrida contends that it is because auto-eroticism appears to enable the philosopher to 'make present' a string of absent love objects in imaginary or symbolic form: Rousseau's memories, desires and wishes about the various women in his life can be instantly activated, and satisfied, in auto-erotic fantasy in a way that could never happen in real life. For Derrida, in other words, it is clear that what we generally take to be the sign of the futility of onanism – the fact that it never involves anyone from the world outside the subject – is rather the guarantee of its total fulfilment (p. 154/221). In Rousseau's case, masturbation is the purest form of sexual pleasure because it collapses the spatio-temporal gap between presence and absence, symbol and reality, desire and gratification into the pure present of auto-erotic pleasure.

There is No Presence

For Rousseau, in other words, masturbation enables him to experience present pleasure more fully than he could ever hope to do in
hetero-erotic relations: this is why the philosopher abandons the 'real'
world of sexual relations with all its contingency, variability and risk in
favour of the assured, instant and total gratification of auto-eroticism.
Yet, it remains the case that Rousseau is *still* sexually frustrated despite
this retreat into the world of pure auto-affection. As Derrida goes on
to argue, the reason for this is that the immediate 'present' delivered
to him in the form of auto-erotic fantasy is, of course, nothing but an
illusion: Rousseau realises that the signs that substitute for the absence
of real women in the philosopher's sex life remain just signs
(p. 154/221). So, upon Derrida's reading, Rousseau's auto-erotic
experience epitomises what he calls the logic of the supplement: what
arrives on the scene to add to, or *enrich*, a supposedly pure presence
also reveals – by virtue of its very necessity – that pure presence *has
never existed*. If masturbatory fantasy is the only way of experiencing
the pure pleasure that can never be delivered up by real life, this is
another way of saying that there is no pure pleasure as such. In other
words, the very thing that appears to give access to pure and immediate presence – the supplement – is also what ensures that presence
will never be given as such: 'something promises itself as it hides itself,
gives itself as it moves itself away, and strictly speaking it cannot even
be called presence' (p. 154/222, translation modified).

Pure Presence is Death

Finally, however, Derrida argues that masturbation plays one more
unusual role within Rousseau's life and text: what starts out as a dangerous *supplement* to the full presence of sex with women paradoxically
ends up as a form of *protection* against a certain danger within this form
of presence itself. It is revealing that Rousseau ultimately comes to see
auto-eroticism less as a waste of natural energy and more as a means
of safeguarding his hypersensitive nature against the dangerously
unmitigated pleasure of sex with women: self-abuse turns out to be a
form of self-preservation. According to his *Confessions*, the philosopher
abstains from 'cohabitation with women' altogether in his middle age
on the grounds that the intensity of the experience might damage his
fragile health or even kill him.[18] For Derrida, Rousseau's recourse to

masturbation as an act of protection against the perils of a real, live sexual encounter with another person once again reveals a certain frailty or insufficiency within pure, unmediated 'presence'. What is supposedly 'natural' or 'healthy' is actually a form of sickness that we need to immunise ourselves against. Yet, why is pure presence equated with sickness, or even death, as opposed to life, fullness or plenitude? To embrace presence is to reject life itself. If we could ever really experience pure presence *as such* – something that was absolutely and unchangingly present in space and time – Derrida argues that this could only be because that thing was entirely lacking in duration, movement, difference, in short, life: this is why Rousseau himself recognises that 'presence' is merely another name for death (p. 155/223). So, Derrida concludes that Rousseau's *Confessions* do not merely tell us about their author's own peculiar personality but rather reveal something about the inherently differential nature of 'presence' itself. In Derrida's words, the point is not so much that Rousseau *prefers* the 'supplement' of auto-eroticism to real sexual experience but rather that 'reality' can *only* be experienced at one remove through the auto-erotic supplement: 'hetero-eroticism . . . can be lived . . . only through the ability to reserve within itself its own supplementary protection' (p. 155/223).

The Supplement Produces 'Presence'

What exactly is taking place here? According to Derrida, Rousseau's entire life story is nothing but a procession from one supplement to another: the philosopher's dead mother is substituted by a beloved foster mother he calls 'Mamma'; Mamma is, in turn, succeeded by his long-term companion Thérèse le Vasseur; education likewise cultivates raw nature, masturbation replaces sex and so on. Of course, we must not forget the most important supplement of all: Rousseau's very act of *writing down* the story of his life in a book, he tells us, is intended to correct the fundamental untrustworthiness of the spoken word. However, what is of interest here is less the individual supplements themselves than *why* they exist in the first place: Derrida's proposition is that the supplement does not add to what was once a pure or complete presence but rather *compensates* for a 'presence' that never actually existed in the first place. To put it in a word, Derrida's now very familiar argument is that the 'supplement' is *originary*: what appears to be a pure or complete moment of presence once again depends for any identity it may possess on its relation to other elements that are not simply present. If such a pure, self-sufficient moment of presence – whether we call it nature, or speech, or sexuality – ever existed, there would no need to produce endless chains of supplements to compensate for its deficiencies. For Derrida, then, it is not that the supplement mediates a pre-existing presence but rather that the supplementary mediations *produce* the illusion of the very thing they supplement: what creates the impression of a fully present 'Mamma' is her supplementation by 'Thérèse', in other words, what produces 'nature' is 'education', what produces 'sex' is 'masturbation' and, of course, what produces 'speech' is 'writing' (p. 157/226). In each case, the impression of absolute and immediate presence is generated by *mediation* itself: 'Immediacy is derived' (p. 157/226).

The Exorbitant

Finally, we must turn to what is now generally agreed to be one of the most important sections of the *Grammatology*: 'The Exorbitant: Question of Method'. It is in this short essay, which is sandwiched between two larger readings of Rousseau, that Derrida offers his most systematic account of his working methodology, so it will repay close attention. As we have seen in the preceding chapters of this book, Derrida's argument has been conducted through a series of often minutely detailed close readings of texts by Saussure, Lévi-Strauss and now Rousseau. Unfortunately, the danger of this forensic approach is, crudely speaking, that we can no longer see the wood for the trees. To clarify his position, then, Derrida steps back from the minutiae of his individual readings to offer a rationale of his methodology: why read Rousseau, or Saussure, or Lévi-Strauss, or anyone in this particular way? If this essay is very interesting on its own terms, however, it is also interesting to note that 'The Exorbitant' anticipates and rebuts what have gone on to become the most enduring if misplaced criticisms of Derrida's philosophy: Derrida believes in nothing, for instance, or Derrida thinks that he is entitled to say anything about anything or Derrida wants to reduce everything in the real world to mere language or 'textuality'. What, then, is Derrida's working methodology? Is he arguing that Rousseau is deliberately or consciously exploring the logic of supplementation established here, for instance, or is he suggesting that there are larger forces at work which go beyond his conscious intention? To what extent, more generally, is Derrida justified in making vast claims about the nature of presence, identity and difference on the basis of a few autobiographical and, heavily idiosyncratic, texts by one historical figure?

Reading

To begin with, Derrida reflects upon the reading he has just offered: what *exactly* does he mean when he talks about 'the logic of the supplement' in Rousseau's texts? It should be pretty clear by now that Derrida is not suggesting that Rousseau is deliberately, consciously or voluntarily articulating the position we have been tracing above. On the contrary, it seems that the eighteenth-century philosopher is never wholly in control of this logic: we have seen how he tacks back and forth between two quite contradictory interpretations of supplementation. For Derrida, Rousseau always ends up saying 'more, less, or something other than what he *would mean* [*voudrait dire*]' (p. 158/226) when he speaks of the supplement. Yet why is there such a gap between what Rousseau means and what he says? To answer this question we need to think about the nature of language itself. If a writer wants to say anything at all, Derrida argues that they must participate within a language whose rules, systems and logic they did not invent and cannot wholly control: we must obey the laws of English or French, for example, if we want to communicate our own intentions to our readers. In Derrida's account, any act of reading is thus a delicate balancing act between respecting how the writer *uses* language to communicate his intentions, on the one hand, and noticing how language continuously *exceeds* the grasp of the writer, on the other. What form does this 'double' reading take?

Double Reading

On the one hand, any act of critical reading must involve a '*doubling commentary* [*commentaire redoublant*]' of the kind that books like this one attempt to provide. We must seek, in other words, to reproduce as faithfully as possible the 'conscious, voluntary, intentional relationship' that every author of a text sets in motion (p. 58/227). Every aspiring reader must thus conform to the traditional academic standards by which such readings are produced: scholarly knowledge must be demonstrated, evidence must be accumulated and readings verified. Indeed, Derrida goes as far as to say that the classical rules of scholarly engagement are 'an indispensable guardrail [*cet indispensable garde-fou*]' (p. 158/227) for readers: without them we would succumb to the kind of free-for-all that would enable us to say whatever we like about a text without danger of refutation. To clear up one very long-standing misconception, then, Derrida is *not* an intellectual relativist: he emphatically does not believe that 'anything goes' in the act of reading, that all readings are equally valid, that there is no such thing as a misreading.[19] However, this kind of faithful or respectful commentary is, for all its importance, still only the *first* step that a double reading must take. If we restricted ourselves to merely reproducing authorial intentionality – whatever Rousseau or any other author meant to say and nothing more – it would quickly become impossible to say anything new, original or surprising about a text. On the other hand, then, a critical reading must also go *beyond* whatever an author may say or mean to say within his/her own texts and identify the complex of forces within every text that exceeds or over-takes (*sur-prises*) authorial intentionality. What exactly does Derrida mean by this 'beyond' though?

The Inside and the Outside
At first glance, a number of obvious answers might suggest themselves. It might well seem, for instance, that Derrida is proposing that we look beyond the confines of the text itself to something in the 'outside' world that would help to explain its meaning: the text's historical context, for example, or the philosophical tradition from which it emerges, or the life or psychology of the person who wrote it. True enough, Rousseau's *Confessions* would seem to be particularly open to what Derrida calls a 'psychobiographical' interpretation: we can easily imagine what Freud, for instance, would make of the eighteenth-century philosopher's peculiar obsession with 'Mamma' and his constant search for mother-supplements. Likewise, Derrida's claim that Rousseau always ends up saying something 'other' than what he consciously intends when speaking of the supplement might seem to be a direct reference to the author's *unconscious* drives or desires. Unfortunately, Derrida is absolutely clear that the kind of reading he has in mind is *not* a psychoanalytic one that tries to go beyond the text

in order to focus on the psyche of its author. If Derrida's working methodology may often look somewhat Freudian – because he is always seeking to bring to the surface a certain 'repressed' element within logocentrism – we have already seen that he remains suspicious of a residually metaphysical dimension within psychoanalysis that leads it to see the text as merely a *symptom* of some psycho-biographical condition in the outside world (p. 159/228). For Derrida, the problem with psychoanalysis and any other reading that seeks to refer to the world 'beyond' the text is that it flies in the face of what we have seen to be the *inextricable* relationship between the signifier and the signified: we can never gain access to a 'transcendental signified' – a mythical beyond – that exists in and of itself independently of all signifiers (p. 159/229). In other words, everything that psychoanalysis and other such methodologies presumes lies *outside* language – the unconscious, sexuality, history, the real world – cannot be divorced from language itself.

There is No Outside-text

To put it in Derrida's own most famous or notorious words, '*there is no outside-text [il n'y a pas de hors-texte]*' (p. 158/227, translation modified). It is difficult to know what to make of this undoubtedly dramatic proposition on first reading. Understandably, its meaning has been hotly debated down the years.[20] At face value, for instance, it may seem that Derrida is claiming that literally nothing exists except language, for instance, or that language is somehow the only reality. However, this would be a very premature conclusion. Let's try to follow what Derrida himself says:

1. First of all, Derrida gives a very simple reason why we cannot say anything about the world 'beyond' the text of the *Confessions*: Rousseau's world is now gone forever. We cannot know what was going through the philosopher's mind when he wrote his autobiography, in other words, or whether his account of his life is a fair and true one. In a very simple sense, then, the only Rousseau we can now know is the one who presents himself *through* texts: there is no longer any Rousseau outside of these texts.

2. Yet, as true as this may be, this is not really what Derrida means when he says that there is no outside-text. It is not simply that the real,

living and breathing Rousseau is gone forever and that all we have left are his texts. According to Derrida, we can go further still: the 'real' Rousseau was always a text even when he was alive! For Derrida, 'there has never been anything but writing' *even* when we speak of Rousseau's real life (p. 159/228). If this seems to be a shockingly counter-intuitive claim at face value – is Derrida somehow saying that 'Rousseau' was never anything more than a word? – it actually follows logically from the critique of presence we have been tracing throughout this book: mediation, difference and writing go all the way down.

3. We still need to be very careful to separate the 'warp' from the 'woof' of Derrida's argument here. It would be quite wrong, for instance, to conclude that he is simply denying the existence of the 'real' Rousseau or asserting that he was only ever a character in a book. Rather, he is arguing that Rousseau's real life was structured according to the principles of mediation, difference and relation that we associate with writing: reality *is* textual. Quite simply, Rousseau did not exist in a sort of vacuum: his life, his thought, his identity, his relations to other people and so on were all embedded within, and constructed out of, a network of different kinds of texts whether linguistic, historical, social, political, sexual and so on.[21] If we put it this way, we can see that Derrida's claim is really just an extension of the argument we have witnessed at work throughout the *Grammatology*: we can have no pure, unmediated experience of presence because all experience is filtered through the network of differential references that is variously named *arche*-writing, the originary trace, *différance* or the supplement.

4. For Derrida, then, it is once again clear that we cannot simply draw a line between 'language' on the one side and the 'world' on the other as if one were more real or authentic than the other. On the contrary, what he calls *arche*- or generalised writing occupies *both* sides of this equation. Writing is not simply restricted to a set of words on a page, in other words, but spills over into what we like to think of as the 'real' world: identity, sexuality, the body and so on are never present in themselves because they are all structured textually. As we saw in Derrida's readings of Husserl, Saussure and Lévi-Strauss, everything that metaphysical philosophy seeks to posit as a pure, unmediated 'presence' that exists in and of itself – whether it be our own subjective consciousness or some object in the world outside

us – turns out to be shot through with difference, relation and mediation. If there is a difference between a work of literary or philosophical biography such as the *Confessions* and the real world outside that work, then, it is not that one is a text and the other is not: both operate according to the same principles. In Derrida's view, Rousseau's *Confessions* merely make visible or manifest the *inherent* textuality of the real Rousseau.

In summary, then, Derrida's claim that '*il n'y a pas de hors-texte*' is neither an attempt to assert that language is the only reality nor to deny the existence of reality per se but rather to stress the impossibility of gaining access to any pure or immediate presence that exists wholly *independently* of the processes of difference and deferral: Rousseau was never purely or simply 'there' in the first place.

The Exorbitant

What, then, does Derrida's own act of reading aim at? Clearly, he is satisfied neither with an act of commentary that just reproduces the *internal* structure of a text, nor with the kind of critique that seeks to view a text from some *external* vantage point, but what he *does* want to do is less than obvious. At the end of the essay, he speaks of wishing to reach a point of 'exteriority' (p. 161/231) with respect to logocentrism but, given his emphatic rejection of psychoanalysis and similar discourses, what this 'outside' might look like remains unclear. To clarify his position, Derrida goes on to argue that his methodology is neither inside nor outside but rather '*exorbitant*' (pp. 161–2/231–2) with respect to metaphysics. Let's conclude by unpacking what he means by this term:

1. First of all, Derrida's reading of Rousseau is certainly 'exorbitant' in the everyday sense of something that is excessive, unjustifiable or disproportionate. As Derrida himself admits, he has no absolutely compelling reason for according such enormous significance to Rousseau rather than anyone else in the history of metaphysics and, without this, his choice can only be arbitrary. Worse still, there is not even a very good justification for focusing on these particular *texts* within the Rousseau canon: why, for instance, does Derrida go on to devote a massively detailed analysis to one short, minor, work entitled

Essay on the Origin of Languages rather than much better-known texts like *Émile* or the *Social Contract?* In this sense, Derrida recognises that for many readers his analysis will look vulnerable to the charge of a crude or naïve empiricism: it seems to reject systematic rational justification altogether in favour of following gut instinct, hunch or even whim.

2. However, there is another, more radical, sense in which Derrida's work is 'exorbitant' in relation to metaphysics. It may well appear that his strategy is empiricist rather than rational but this is not quite the whole story. As he has already shown in his critique of structuralism, what philosophy derides as 'empiricism' is not actually non-philosophical at all because it only has meaning *within* the conceptual oppositions determined by metaphysics itself: the rational versus the empirical, the theoretical versus the practical and, more generally, the 'philosophical' versus the 'non-philosophical'. If it seems that empiricism is somehow 'outside' metaphysics, in other words, it actually remains a metaphysical concept through and through: empiricism is philosophy's *own* idea of what non-philosophy should look like. For Derrida, then, it is clear that, in order to truly go 'beyond' metaphysics, we need to exceed *both* everything within that system and everything that the system posits as its own outside.

3. To Derrida's eyes, then, the 'exorbitant' is not so much an excessive, disproportionate or unphilosophical methodology as a more radical attempt to *exceed* the entire *orbit* (*ex-orbis*) of the metaphysics of presence (p. 162/231). Consequently, it follows that any such method is, by definition, indescribable by any of the conceptual oppositions that circulate within that orbit, even or especially the opposition between the philosophical and the non-philosophical. For Derrida, his inability to offer an absolute justification for his own reading is neither a rejection of theory nor an embrace of practice but rather the upshot of his attempt to question the metaphysical desire for an absolute ground, origin or foundation on which to base all knowledge. In the absence of any true point of origin, we must begin '*wherever we are*' he writes, because the thought of the 'originary' trace has already taught us that it is 'impossible to justify a point of departure absolutely' (p. 162/233).

4. So, we must begin wherever we find ourselves, then, and for Derrida in *Of Grammatology* that place just happens to be Rousseau's texts and, more precisely, the figure of the 'supplement'. Of course,

it is no more possible to justify his focus on this particular figure than any other aspect of his reading: we could easily substitute someone or something else in its stead. At best, we might say that what justifies the decision to focus on the 'supplement' is that this possibility of substitutability is *built into* the very figure itself: the supplement is already a substitute in the first place. For Derrida, though, the crucial question is less *which* specific supplement comes to stand in for a supposed presence – it could be education, masturbation, writing or anything – but rather *why* such a supplement is necessary. We already know his answer: there never was any full presence in the first place. In this sense, Derrida's starting point may be arbitrary and provisional but his ultimate goal is always the same: to reveal the inherent supplementarity of *all* 'presence'.

For Derrida, then, we might say that the 'supplement' is exorbitant in every sense of the term. It is a kind of structural 'blindspot [*tâche aveugle*]' that resists every attempt to explain it with reference to the categories of metaphysics (p. 163/234). Accordingly, we can see the supplement as neither an addition nor a substitute, neither good nor evil, neither passive nor active, neither a conscious theme in Rousseau's text nor a manifestation of the unconscious of the author, neither within the enclosure of the text itself, nor 'outside' it in some, supposedly extra-textual, 'real' world. To Derrida's way of thinking, any attempt to trace the figure of the supplement in Rousseau's texts must push straight through all these inherently metaphysical sets of oppositions precisely because the logic of supplementation *is what makes each of them possible* in the first place: each requires supplementation by its opposite in order to be what it is to start with. However, if this state of affairs radically transforms what we understand by Rousseau and his texts, it also compels us to reflect back on ourselves and our own act of reading. If there is 'nothing outside of the text', then there can be no question of Derrida (or anyone else) merely observing this logic of supplementation in Rousseau's texts from the 'outside': we all have our own blindspots. The fact is that *every* text is the product of a logic of difference, relation or supplementarity that exceeds its author's control. This is why every text, whether it be Rousseau's reading of his own life, Derrida's reading of Rousseau or even our own reading of Derrida, will always mean something more, less or *other* than what it would mean. In this sense, we might say that Derrida's 'exorbitant' question of method necessarily exceeds all of us (p. 164/234).

Conclusion

What, then, has Derrida achieved at this stage of his reading of Rousseau? We now know what an exorbitant reading of Rousseau looks like in 'theory' (if we can still use that term) but we still need to see what form it takes in practice. As we will see in the following section of this book, the main business of Part II of the *Grammatology* is an examination of how the logic of the supplement operates in just one short essay by Rousseau: *The Essay on the Origin of Languages*. To be sure, Derrida's reading of Rousseau is 'exorbitant' in the everyday sense of that term: it is a massively, almost excessively, detailed piece of analysis that is considerably longer than the essay it analyses. However, this reading of the *Essay* is also 'ex-orbitant' in the specialised sense of that term we have just been articulating. If Derrida's reading is excessive, in other words, what it attempts to exceed are not simply scholarly norms and expectations but the 'orbit' of metaphysics itself together with all the oppositions that animate Rousseau's text: nature versus culture, good versus evil and, of course, speech versus writing. In Derrida's account, we will see that Rousseau's *Essay on the Origin of Languages* contains a logic of the supplement that exceeds not simply language but even the very idea of the 'origin' itself.

Rousseau and the Origin(s) of Language

In what remains of Part II of the *Grammatology* – Chapters 3 and 4 – Derrida offers a long and extremely detailed reading of Rousseau's *Essay on the Origin of Languages*. It is here that the complex argument about presence, writing and difference we have traced throughout this work is given its fullest and most expansive treatment. As we will see, Derrida's aim in this chapter is to analyse what he calls a 'logic of the supplement' at work within Rousseau's attempt to trace language all the way back to the first inarticulate cry of passion in the state of nature. To Derrida's way of thinking, of course, the 'origin' of language does not lie in a simple moment of presence but in a state of originary difference, relation or supplementation: *in the beginning was the supplement*. If Rousseau tries to tell the story of language's degeneration from the natural cry of passion to the precise, cold and abstract written word, in other words, Derrida will once again demonstrate that this is less a decline and fall *from* the state of nature than a crisis *within* the natural itself: everything that the eighteenth-century philosopher presents as a deviation from language's natural origins, in other words, will be shown to be always already 'present' from the very beginning. What, then, does Derrida have to say about Rousseau? How does he trace the logic of the supplement in his theory of language? To what extent can we detect this originary complexity or self-division at the heart of language? For Derrida, as we will see, there is no origin of language as such.

Rousseau and the Origin of Language

First, however, I want to briefly introduce Derrida's self-professedly 'exorbitant' reading of the *Essay on the Origin of Languages*. Unfortunately, we won't be able to cover every single aspect of Derrida's reading here: the chapter on the *Essay* is substantial enough to be a separate book in itself. As any new reader quickly appreciates, this is a *tour-de-force* of Rousseau scholarship: Derrida has many important things to say about the historical composition of Rousseau's *Essay* (whether all the chapters were written at the same time), its place within the corpus of his major works (whether it was written before or after the second *Discourse*) and its contribution to contemporary philosophical debates about pity, music and other issues. To do Derrida's argument any justice, we will restrict ourselves to just three aspects of his reading of Rousseau: his account of music, language, and finally, his tantalising but incomplete theory of writing. Yet, even so, the basic thrust of Derrida's argument will be very familiar to us by now. For Derrida, as we saw in the previous section, it is not a question of repeating the internal argument of the text or rejecting it in favour of some non-textual outside but of identifying a point of 'exorbitancy': what he strives for is something that *exceeds* the text but from *within* its own perimeters. If Derrida's aim is to offer a 'double reading' of Rousseau's *Essay*, in other words, this reading will always remain embedded within the logic, discourse and argument of the text itself: the Rousseau who officially champions passion, speech and melody will, once again, be pitted against the Rousseau who surreptitiously but unmistakably supports need, writing and harmony. In this sense, we will again see that Rousseau's *Essay* is an example, if an extremely privileged one, of what we have called 'metaphysics in deconstruction'.

In his little-known *Essay on the Origins of Languages in which something is said about Melody and Musical Imitation*, Jean-Jacques Rousseau seeks to offer a historical account of the evolution of language from its beginnings in inarticulate speech to the present day.

To summarise his general argument, Rousseau contends that humanity invented the spoken word not in order to express our physical needs – hunger, thirst, warmth and so on – but our *passions*: 'love, hatred, pity, anger wrung the first voices out of them' (*Discourses*, p. 253). As human culture evolved, however, a new, more precise form of language was required to articulate abstract ideas as well as feelings and this was writing. In Rousseau's account, though, the invention of the written word represented a fall or degeneration from the sensible purity of an oral community: writing buys a greater precision but only at the expense of the immediacy and expressiveness of speech.

The middle sections of the *Essay* turn from the question of the origin of language in general to the origin of particular languages. Again, Rousseau draws an important distinction, but this time it is between languages of the north and south. On the one side, 'southern' languages are said to spring from passion: the warm climate, fertile soil and conditions in Southern Europe and Africa provide man with everything he needs to subsist so he only has to use language in order to express his desires. On the other, however, 'northern' languages are deemed to be the result of direct physical need: the cold climate, poor earth and meagre conditions in northern Europe mean that language developed first and foremost as a way of surviving. In Rousseau's pithy summation, the first words of southern man were 'love me' (*aimez-moi*) whereas the first words of northern man were 'help me' (*aidez-moi*) (p. 279).

Finally, Rousseau's *Essay* explores all these questions from a different perspective by considering the origin of music. He argues that language and music share a common origin because both are direct vocal expressions of our passions. Once again, however,

Rousseau makes an important distinction between two different modes of music: melody and harmony. If melody is the pure expression of our passions, the evolution of harmony introduces a fatal complexity, abstraction and artificiality into music. Just as the written word sacrifices the passion of speech for greater precision of expression, so harmony surrenders the pure and immediate expressiveness of melody in favour of elaborate but lifeless harmonic arrangements (pp. 295–8). In this way, Rousseau's account of the degeneration of music mirrors his larger critique of the degeneration of human society from the primitive utopia that was the state of nature.

What is the hermeneutical key with which Derrida attempts to unlock Rousseau's essay? Of course, it is once again the logic of the *supplement*. As we saw in the previous chapter, Rousseau's *Confessions* is the story of the movement from one supplement to another: the originary presence of speech is supplemented by writing, nature by culture, interiority by exteriority, sex by masturbation and so on endlessly. For Rousseau himself, of course, each supplement is nothing more than a pure addition to an origin that is already fully present in itself: what is added is quite literally *nothing* – a spare part – because the origin itself does not need anything to complete it (p. 167/238). However, the obvious question that follows from here is – if the origin requires no supplement and the supplement adds nothing to the origin – then *why* does the supplement ever come into existence, why is it necessary? The answer Derrida supplies is that the 'fully present origin' which has no need of supplementation never existed in the first place. This pure and simple 'origin', which is supposedly complete in itself, is nothing but the attempt to erase or annul the originary trace or *différance*. In his reading of the *Essay on the Origin of Language*, Derrida will trace this double logic of the supplement (where it is both an addition to, and a compensation for a lack within, presence) through a network of new oppositions in Rousseau's thought: passion versus need, freedom versus enslavement, south versus north, melody versus harmony and so on.

The Origin of Music

Second, Derrida turns to an analysis of just one section of Rousseau's essay: his account of the history of music. According to Derrida, this relatively brief discussion, which does not even begin until Chapter 12 of the *Essay*, is not just the postscript that some scholars have taken it to be. On the contrary, it is the 'major preoccupation' of Rousseau's text (p. 195/279) because the story of language is intimately bound up with the story of music: both begin as ways of giving voice to our passions. To put it in Rousseau's own words: 'passion rouses all of the [vocal] organs' and so song and speech have 'a common origin' (*Discourses*, p. 282). If language and music have the same origin, however, they also share the same fate: what begins as a simple expression of passion quickly degenerates into a cold, abstract and expressionless form. For Rousseau, the story of the decline and fall of music from the state of nature is the story of the fall from melody into harmony.

Melody and Harmony

It is important to get to grips with this distinction before we go any further because it will play an instrumental role in Derrida's critique. According to music theory, what is called musical 'pitch' – the perceived frequency of any given sound – can be sub-divided into the categories of 'melody' and 'harmony'. To put it very crudely, melody and harmony are primarily distinguished by *number*. On the one side, for instance, a melody is a series or sequence of single sounds: a melodic pattern will obviously contain changes or modulations, but it must be perceived as *a single sonic* entity or line. On the other, however, a harmony is a combination of sounds that are performed simultaneously at separate pitches in the form of, say, chords: a C chord, for example, comprises the three notes C, E and G performed together. If a melody is essentially monophonic (single-voiced), a harmony is polyphonic: it depends upon the perceived *interplay* between what are technically called 'intervals', that is, different sounds operating at different pitches. In structural terms, then, harmony is obviously more complex than melody: it could not be performed by a single voice because it depends upon the intervals – the spaces or differences – between a number of voices.

From Melody to Harmony

Upon Rousseau's reading, then, the first form of music can only have been melody. It is melody, as a monophonic sequence of pure sounds, that is closest to the cry of passion that, for the philosopher, represents the origin of language: 'melody expresses plaints, cries of suffering or of joy, threats, moans' (*Discourses*, p. 287). Inasmuch as it involves a complex interplay of sounds, harmony is obviously at one remove from this state of nature: 'what have chords in common with our passions?' he rhetorically demands (p. 287). Yet, as is so often the case in the *Grammatology*, what is interesting about Rousseau's account is that the inferior term in a hierarchy will not stay in its rightful place. For Rousseau, harmony does not merely represent an unnecessary addition to the pure expressiveness of melody because it quickly begins to *overtake* melody: it substitutes an artificial, conventional form of expression for the pure expressiveness of melody. Now, the problem with this for Rousseau is that harmony's greater complexity of arrangement is bought at the cost of the life and energy of melody: what begins as the vocalisation of love, anger or pain thus degenerates into an empty, formal or technical exercise. The formal constraint that harmony imposes upon melody replaces pure expression of feeling with the calculation of intervals or differences. This decline and fall reaches its nadir with the kind of elaborate contrapuntal arrangements favoured by contemporary French composers like Rameau. In Rousseau's tragic account, contemporary music has lost all connection with the passions that originally gave it life and degenerated into pure harmony (p. 298).

Harmony Supplements Melody

To Derrida's way of thinking, however, it will be no surprise to learn that the story of the decline and fall from melody into harmony is more complicated than it appears. Of course, we have seen this kind of mythological narrative many times before in the *Grammatology*: what starts out as a simple, full and unified presence (presence, nature, speech, freedom) somehow always ends up being corrupted by the arrival into its midst of some perverse, unnatural foreign body (difference, culture, writing, enslavement). Now, what is consistently represented as *extrinsic* to the state of nature – external, superfluous, unimportant – is actually *intrinsic* to nature's own self-definition,

Derrida shows. For Rousseau, as we have already seen in the previous section, this foreign body is consistently figured as a 'dangerous supplement [*ce supplément dangereux*]' that insinuates its way into, mediates and endangers the original state of nature. We can clearly see this same process at work in his account of music. On the one hand, melody is nothing less than the pure, direct and unmediated voice of nature itself. On the other, though, harmony is a supplement that introduces a layer of mediation, difference and artifice into nature. If harmony is merely an *addition* to the plenitude of melody, which adds nothing and risks taking away everything, then the inevitable question is *why* this wholly unnecessary supplement to nature ever appears in the first place? In Derrida's account, of course, the answer is by now obvious: the supplement does not add to nature but reveal a lack – an originary difference – within the natural itself (*Grammatology*, p. 214/308).

Imitation of Life
For Derrida, Rousseau's history of music is not so much the story of the fall from melody into harmony as a different tale altogether: what the latter calls 'harmony' – an artificial network of differences, spacing and intervals which cuts up the pure stream of sound – is already at work within the natural unity of melody. Let's take this slowly. According to Derrida, a key aspect of Rousseau's aesthetic theory, and indeed of his philosophy more generally, that enables us to unravel the opposition between melody and harmony is the classical idea of imitation or '*mimesis*': what distinguishes any art form, such as music, is the extent to which it imitates or reproduces the natural world. To Rousseau, it is this capacity to perfectly imitate the sounds of our natural passions that makes melody the original form of music:

> By imitating the inflections of the voice, melody expresses plaints, cries of suffering or of joy, threats, moans; all the vocal signs of the passions fall within its province. It imitates the accents of [various] languages as well as the idiomatic expressions commonly associated in each one of them with given movements of the soul. (*Discourses*, p. 287)

We can, however, begin to detect a contradiction in the overall argument of the *Discourse* here. On the one hand, Rousseau has just argued that melody is a pure and direct *expression* of our natural passions. On the other, though, Rousseau now seems to be suggesting that melody is an *imitation* or reproduction of those passions. Now, if melody is an imitation of the voice of nature, even if it is the most exact imitation possible, then it logically follows that it cannot quite be natural: the imitation of a thing cannot, by definition, be the thing itself. So, in Rousseau's own terms, as we will see in a moment, what is supposed to be the direct expression of our natural passions in fact subtly *modifies*, or even, he suggests, *improves* upon, nature itself.

Good and Bad Imitations

We can now begin to see why Rousseau's attempt to narrate the history of music in terms of a simple *fall* from a state of nature into a decadent and artificial culture backfires. The difference between melody and harmony is not so much a matter of kind, where one is natural and the other unnatural, than of degree. As forms of music, both melody and harmony are imitations of nature rather than direct expressions of the voice of nature itself. In order to shore up his original thesis, Rousseau is thus forced to fall back on a much finer distinction between a 'good' form of imitation (which is utterly faithful to natural law) and a 'bad' form of imitation (which distorts and falsifies this law). On the one side, for instance, he attempts to praise imitation as intrinsic to human nature: it distinguishes us from animals, enables us to communicate our natural sympathy for others, and lays the foundations for education, art and culture. On the other, however, he also wants to castigate imitation as a perversion of our essential humanity: it interrupts natural simplicity or spontaneity, introduces vice and duplicity into our relations with others and corrupts art, culture and society by making possible inequality, decadence, and empty formalism. Yet, can Rousseau have his mimetic cake and eat it, so to speak? If *all* imitation creates a gap between nature and culture, the sign and the reality, the original and the copy, then the question is whether we can then go on to make this kind of qualitative distinction between 'good' and 'bad' copies on the grounds that one is more natural than the other. For Derrida, the very possibility of imitation 'assures a lodging for falsehood, falsification, and vice': the 'good' copy always carries within it the threat of the 'bad' copy (*Grammatology*, p. 205/292).

Melody is Harmony
What, then, are the implications of Rousseau's mimetic theory for the opposition between melody and harmony? It goes without saying that, if everything he says about imitation being the basis of art holds true, the philosopher cannot make good his attempt to differentiate between melody and harmony on the grounds that the one is natural and the other cultural: *both* are unnatural. Thus, he is forced to concede that the relationship between the two is much closer than he first suggested: any melody – considered purely as a modulating sequence of sounds on a scale – *already* has its basis in harmony (p. 212/303). However, the philosopher tries to shore up his crumbling position by, once again, retreating to a much finer distinction between what he calls 'good' and 'bad' melodic form. For Rousseau, as we will already have guessed from the discussion of *mimesis* above, what distinguishes the superior form of melody from its inferior, harmonic, equivalent, is that it *faithfully imitates* the passionate voice of nature itself as opposed to *falsifying* or *interrupting* that natural condition. Now, we can applaud Rousseau's exhaustive attempts to re-establish the opposition between melody and harmony, however, without taking them at face value. If the philosopher argues that melody represents a 'good' form of imitation, which stands in contrast to the 'bad' form that is harmony, the objection that Derrida presented above still stands. The problem is that imitation – whether good or bad, faithful or unfaithful, natural or unnatural – 'has always already interrupted natural plenitude' by the very fact of its existence. This means that Rousseau's attempt to distinguish between degrees of imitation is doing nothing more than splitting hairs (p. 215/308). In spite of Rousseau's protestations to the contrary, his own argument makes it abundantly clear that melody is no more a simple or faithful imitation of nature than harmony: melody 'not only imitates, it speaks; and its language, though inarticulate, is lively, ardent and a hundred times more vigorous than speech itself' (*Discourses*, p. 287).

The Non-origin of Music
In his provisional conclusion, Derrida proposes that Rousseau's account of the history of music is another example of what we have called the logic of the supplement at work in his texts: what holds for the relation between sex and masturbation also holds for the

relationship between melody and harmony. Of course, Rousseau sees harmony as a mere 'supplement' to the natural plenitude of melody: the invention of the harmonic form of music is an – at best superfluous and at worst dangerous – addition to the original and self-sufficient state of nature. What the logic of the supplement insists, though, is that harmony is not simply something that is super-added to an original moment of pure presence but rather something that reveals an inherent lack within what should be that moment of presence. To put it in a nutshell, what Rousseau calls 'nature' is not complete in itself but is rather an originary deficiency – a non-identity, mediation or *différance* – that *demands* supplementation by imitation:

[I]n every imitation, some sort of discourse must always complement the voice of nature. A musician who tries to render noise with noise errs; he knows neither the weaknesses nor the strengths of his art; he judges of it without taste or insight; teach him that he must render noise with song, that if he wished to make frogs croak he would have to make them sing; for it is not enough for him merely to imitate, he must do so in a way that both moves and pleases, otherwise his dreary imitation is as nought, and by failing to arouse anyone's interest, it fails to make any impression. (*Discourse*, p. 288)

For Derrida, then, it is clear that everything Rousseau seeks to *oppose* to the pure and unmediated voice of nature – harmony, imitation, culture, society – exists in order to supply, correct, or compensate for, what increasingly looks like an inherent deficiency, which in the above passage is figured as a rawness, ugliness or noise, within that voice that calls for supplementation: what seems to belong *outside* nature is, as we have seen throughout this book, always already working *within* it in order to make it what it should be in the first place. What implications, then, does this 'becoming-supplemental' of nature itself hold for Rousseau's theory of the origin of language?

The Origin of Language

Third, Derrida turns to an analysis of the main task of Rousseau's *Essay*: an attempt to write a history of the origin, evolution and ultimate degeneration of language. Unfortunately, we will not be able to follow every path within this long and detailed argument so we will again restrict ourselves to tracing the contours of Derrida's argument. Once again, what Derrida is trying to do here is to identify a point of 'exorbitancy' in Rousseau's text where the philosopher's declared aims or intentions are overtaken or surprised by larger forces. For Derrida, it is this gap between what Rousseau *declares* and what he actually *describes* – what he means to say and what he cannot help but say – that is the site of his own reading. If Rousseau's history of language is organised around a set of oppositions and hierarchies – north versus south, need versus passion, articulation versus accent – Derrida will once again show how each of these opposed terms inheres in its other: what begin as absolute differences and hierarchies unravel into a field of traces, spaces and relations. In this way, Derrida will build up to his major point about Rousseau's essay: there is no absolute origin of language as such.

North and South

It is necessary to go back to the founding premise of Rousseau's own argument to grasp Derrida's point: language originates in *passion* rather than need. We first spoke in order to express our love, anger, pity rather than our hunger, thirst or coldness. As we have already seen, the *Essay* goes on to argue that this opposition between passion and need is reflected in the difference between northern and southern tongues. In the warm, southern hemisphere, language is the expression of passion: the first words of the man of the south were 'love me'. In the cold, northern hemisphere, language is dictated by pure need: the first words of the northern man were 'help me' (p. 279). To Rousseau's way of thinking, it thus follows that southern languages are closer to the true origin of language in the cry of passion: what he calls the 'south' is nothing less than the cradle of language itself. If we move northwards up the globe, we thus move further and further away from language in its original state. This is why Rousseau sees the gradual emergence of a cold, northern language of utility as a process of perversion or corruption. So, for Rousseau, in other words, it becomes clear that the difference between the North and South Poles is not simply a geographical distinction but a linguistic, political and ultimately a *moral* one: the degeneration of language in modernity is, put another way, nothing less than the becoming-North of the whole globe.

According to Derrida, however, what Rousseau actually describes – as opposed to what he declares to be the case – constantly works to undermine this set of oppositions between north and south, need and passion and so on. It is clear, to begin with, that Rousseau's geographical claim militates against his larger linguistic, political and moral purpose. Quite simply, what defines the geography of the globe is its mobility: the world turns on its axis, seasons change and all positions – north, south, east and west – exist in relation to other positions. Yet, Rousseau's account of the origin of language tries to *freeze* this essential relativity and variability into a set of static, absolute differences. Every language is assigned an absolutely fixed position on the globe – either the North Pole or the South Pole – as if no position between these two extremities could possibly exist! For Derrida, in other words, Rousseau's attempt to claim that the true origin of language lies in a so-called absolute South is at odds with what it describes: we cannot say that any language is absolutely 'northern' or 'southern' because languages have, at best, a relative position in the world. If Rousseau seeks to distinguish categorically between northern and southern languages, Derrida's argument is that this distinction is rather a question of degree: we can speak of languages that are more 'northern' and less 'southern' – more passionate and less necessary – but we cannot make any absolute distinction between the two. In this sense, what Rousseau's attempt to distinguish between north and south actually describes is not a polar opposition between two diametrically opposed kinds of language but a more subtle, less clear-cut distribution of forces *within* every single language: every language contains elements of both north and south, passion and need (*Grammatology*, p. 217/310).

Passion and Need

To recall Rousseau's central thesis in the *Essay*, all language originates in our *passions*, as opposed to our needs, but even this absolutely fundamental opposition is not as stable as we might think. It is difficult to understand, for instance, how Rousseau can distinguish between southern and northern tongues in terms of passion and need if *all* language is supposed to spring from passion: why do the so-called 'northern' languages exist at all? Upon Derrida's reading, the difference between passion and need, just like the difference between the north and south, is actually internal to every language: every language contains traces of both passion and need. For Derrida, indeed, it is striking that Rousseau's philosophy is not even clear on the very basic question of what *exactly* differentiates a 'need' from a 'passion' in the first place: the eighteenth-century thinker once wrote a fragmentary definition of 'need' which included not only such immediate requirements as sleep, shelter or food but less pressing appetites like sensual pleasure or sex. Now, the problem is that what Rousseau describes here as a basic 'need' – love or sexual desire – has, by the time he comes to write the *Essay*, mysteriously turned into a 'passion': 'love, hatred, pity, anger wrung the first voices out of them' (*Discourses*, p. 253)! If Rousseau's confusion over love seems to imply that need is always present within passion, in a way that completely contradicts his attempt to oppose the two, we can find further evidence to support this thesis in the *Discourse on the Origin of Inequality*. In Part 1 of that essay, for instance, we see the philosopher arguing that, far from being opposed to need, passion *originates* in our wants (*Grammatology*, p. 219/314).What implications does this state of affairs hold for the *Essay on the Origin of Languages*?

We must again turn to the logic of the supplement if we wish to understand the complex relationship between passion, need and language. It is no longer possible to distinguish between languages of passion and need on the grounds that the former are closer to the supposedly natural 'origin' of language than the latter. Rather, we must now speak of an economy or distribution of need and passion rather than a simple opposition because neither can exist in total isolation from the other (p. 225/321). For Derrida, Rousseau's inability to distinguish between languages of need and passion once again points to the presence of an originary supplementation. What Rousseau calls the natural origin of language – passion – is already complex, differentiated, contaminated by what should lie outside it. Now, the possibility that language has, by definition, always had more than one origin poses a real problem for Rousseau's attempt to narrate the history of language as the gradual degeneration that passes from south to north, passion to need and ultimately speech to writing. If languages of the north are dominated by need rather than passion, it cannot be because they represent a perversion of the origin of language itself, in other words, but rather because this possibility of perversity is always present from the outset: Derrida goes to great lengths to show how the language of need is 'forever related' to the language of passion 'persevering in it, submitting to it or controlling it' (p. 223/319).[22] In this sense, we must see the language of need as a supplement to the language of passion in the full sense of that term: what Rousseau calls the 'North' is not somewhere that exists at the furthest remove from the one true origin of language, in other words, but is rather the outworking of 'another origin' that compensates for what the first origin lacks (p. 224/319).

Accent and Articulation

For Derrida, another key problem within Rousseau's *Essay* is the opposition between accent and articulation. This opposition, arguably even more than the one between passion and need, is what enables Rousseau to differentiate the languages of the south from the languages from the north. Upon the eighteenth-century philosopher's reading, southern languages are defined by what he calls 'accent' – liveliness, expressiveness and that certain sonorous or euphonic quality that also marks the beginning of song – whereas northern languages are characterised by what he terms 'articulation' – greater precision and clarity, to be sure, but also the dullness and ugliness that springs from a mode of discourse whose main purpose is utility. Now, Rousseau's story of the growing *articulation* of language, the process of cutting up the pure stream of sound into 'sound-bites' through the introduction of difference, modulation or spacing, is the ultimate basis of his larger narrative about the gradual *degeneration* of language and society more generally. However, Derrida once again seeks to question this mythological account of a fall from a pure, self-present and undifferentiated state of nature into the atomised, divided and unequal world of modern, civic society. If Rousseau typically presents articulation as a degeneration or catastrophe that affects the original condition of language from without, as if the peoples of the northern hemisphere were not human beings at all but aliens from another planet, what his own account again reveals is that the apparent 'supplement' is essential to what it supplements. Just as melody *is* harmony, south *is* north, and passion *is* need, so we will discover that *language is always already articulate from the very beginning* (p. 229/325). In Derrida's account, as we will see later on, this insight has important knock-on effects for Rousseau's theory of writing as well because, for the latter, the defining quality of the written word is nothing other than this articulacy: the claim that all 'language is *articulate*' is thus another way of saying that 'all language is *writing*' (p. 229/326).

What, though, is the basis of Derrida's audacious argument that *all* language *already* contains articulation? It is once more only necessary to measure the gap between what Rousseau declares is the case and what he himself is compelled to describe in order to find the answer.[23] Again, this contradiction expresses itself in the form of the logic of the supplement: what is ideally presented as a mere addition to a full or complete origin turns out to be necessarily present within the origin itself. To Rousseau's way of thinking, of course, we did not originally require articulation in order to express ourselves, but in fact his own account of the evolution of human language suggests the exact opposite is the case: *to speak at all is to articulate*. What he calls the cry of nature, the animal sound that emerges naturally from the throat, is not yet a language (p. 242/344). Yet what is it that turns this primitive animal cry into human language? For Rousseau, the origin of human language does not lie in any particular *organ*, such as the larynx or vocal chords, so much as in the acquisition of the necessary signs, symbols or conventions that enable us to communicate ideas in the form of sounds: '[c]onventional language belongs to man alone' (*Discourses*, p. 252). If human beings must first acquire a repertoire of complex cultural conventions in order to express even our most basis passions – love, anger, pity and so on – then it becomes difficult to see how Rousseau can speak of a 'natural' language at all: the use of conventional language is, on the contrary, precisely what *distinguishes* human life from the natural world. The argument that the pure, inarticulate cry of nature is not yet language in any meaningful sense of the term leads us to the conclusion that what characterises language is nothing other than articulation. This capacity to articulate sound, to cut up the cry of nature up into what Saussure would call a series of phonic signifiers, is the basis of *all* human language whether northern or southern, passionate or necessary. So, in a paradoxical sense, then, what Rousseau presents as the ruination of language – the intervention of difference, spacing, supplementarity in the form of articulation – is actually its condition of possibility: '*language is born out of the process of its own degeneration*' Derrida writes (*Grammatology*, p. 242/344).

The Non-origin of Language

In summary, then, we can see that Derrida finds the same logic of the supplement at work in Rousseau's theory of the origin of language as he did in his theory of music: what should be outside the original state of language, whether we call it 'harmony', 'need' 'articulation' or simply *difference*, is in each case working within the 'origin' from the outset. To put it another way, *everything is articulated*: the kind of differing and deferral in space and time that define articulation are not some sort of accident or catastrophe that befall language from without, so much as its basic and original condition. As Derrida goes on to show, Rousseau's inability to accept this claim leaves his argument impaled on the horns of a contradiction. On the one side, for instance, he continues to declare that articulation is merely an unnecessary addition to the natural state of language that, at best, adds nothing to it, and, at worst, risks enfeebling or corrupting its expressive force. On the other, however, he consistently shows how articulation is already *present* within the so-called 'natural' language, supplying it with the precision it lacks, enabling it to *be* expressive in the first place (p. 246/351). Now, Rousseau is typically ingenious in his attempts to shore up his argument against this basic incoherence – the philosopher again attempts to get around the problem by distinguishing between different *degrees* of articulation in the same way that he earlier differentiated between 'good' and 'bad' forms of imitation and melody – but what he is unable to recognise is *why* this argument continually falls apart.[24] For Derrida, of course, the answer to this question is very simple: what inexorably binds melody and harmony, north and south, passion and need, accent and articulation and presence and absence together – despite Rousseau's best efforts to keep them apart – is nothing other than the logic of the trace, *différance* or supplement (p. 246/351). We are thus now in a position to say what Rousseau's own account is unable to think. The origin of language is always already articulated, shot through with difference, spacing and deferral, and so it follows that language has no pure or simple 'origin' at all. This insight leads Derrida to completely re-write Rousseau's tragic narrative of the decline and fall of language from the originary cry of passion in the state of nature to the cold, mechanical precision of the written word in modernity. What, then, does Derrida have to say about Rousseau's theory of writing?

The Origin of Writing

Finally, Derrida turns to Rousseau's theory of the origin of writing in the concluding chapter of the *Grammatology*. Indeed, we might argue that the whole of Derrida's reading of the *Essay* has been building up to this moment. As we know, Rousseau's text understands the history of language as the progression, or rather regression, from one supplement for the origin to another: harmony supplements melody, articulation replaces accent, etc. To Derrida's eyes, however, it is writing that is the supplement *par excellence* in the *Essay*: what happens when the written word comes on the scene is the final triumph of difference over presence, mediation over immediacy, coldness or death over the life and warmth of speech. For Rousseau, we have seen, writing's greater precision and articulation is bought at the cost of the passion and expression that animated language in the first place: '[W]riting, which might be expected to fix language, is precisely what adulterates it; it changes not its words but its genius; it substitutes precision for expressiveness' (*Discourses*, p. 260). If writing introduces a fatal gap or difference into the act of expression, though, it also creates the social and political division and inequality that marks modern civil society. In Rousseau's account, which is, of course, echoed almost 200 years later by his disciple Lévi-Strauss, the written word divides what was hitherto an equal and unified community, where everyone was within earshot, into two distinct classes of people: the literate and the-non-literate, the governing class and the workers, and so on.

The theory of writing proposed by Rousseau could thus be said to encapsulate the entire history of what Derrida calls 'logocentrism'. Of course, it will be no surprise to learn by now that the latter is intensely sceptical of this narrative of a catastrophic and inexplicable fall from presence into absence, immediacy into mediation and so on: what Rousseau deems to be a fall *from* presence is always a fall *within* a so-called 'presence'. As we have seen throughout this book, it is only necessary to trace the gaps, blindspots or moments of violence in Rousseau's own text, where he yokes fact and interpretation together – to glimpse a counter-narrative to the 'official' story. For Derrida, Rousseau's anxiety to make good his claim about the *belatedness* of writing – its relatively late arrival on the historical scene – forces him to completely re-write history in order to fit with his theory. Derrida shows, for instance, how Rousseau goes to almost absurd lengths to prove that the Ancient Greek poet Homer did not know how to write for the simple reason that any evidence to the contrary would contradict his theory that the epoch of the poem historically preceded the epoch of writing (*Grammatology*, p. 269/379). However, the eighteenth-century philosopher protests too much. If Homer did indeed know how to write, and all the evidence points in this direction,[25] then Rousseau's entire theory of writing begins to fall apart: what is supposed to replace or even *destroy* the pure expressiveness and passion of the spoken word now appears to *co-exist peacefully* with, or alongside, it. In other words, we are confronted with a more complex and general version of 'writing' than the eighteenth-century philosopher allows: this supposedly belated linguistic form is actually present at the very origin of language itself.

This leads us back to where we started. It is only through the logic of the supplement that we can explain the irreconcilable contradictions in Rousseau's account. As we have seen throughout this section, the philosopher's understanding of supplementarity always cuts in two different ways and nowhere is this more true than in relation to the theory of writing. On the one hand, he constantly declares that writing is a mere addition – a spare part – that introduces a fatal mediation, articulation or precision into the pure expressiveness of speech. On the other, however, he continually describes a situation where writing comes to substitute or compensate for a speech that is already lacking in life, immediacy or expressiveness. Quite simply, what writing actually reveals is that that the supposed cry of passion that constitutes the origin of language was *never* pure, intact, complete in the first place: the 'origin' is *itself* a supplement. Of course, Rousseau himself argues that writing substitutes a cold, mechanical exactitude for the pure expressiveness of speech: 'it substitutes precision for expressiveness'. Yet, according to the philosopher's own account, such exactitude was *already* present in speech from the beginning. For Rousseau, as we have already seen, what distinguishes the utterance of the first human word from the simple cry of the animal is nothing other than that very quality of articulation he now seeks to assign to writing alone: *language is articulate from the moment of its birth*. If all language is articulate from the very outset, however, and all articulation just as inevitably leads to writing, then it logically follows that all language might just as easily be called *written*: what the historical invention of the written word comes to replace is, paradoxically enough, not speech or expressiveness but a version of itself

(p. 315/443). The very thing that Rousseau seeks to repress or exclude from language in its most essential or interior state – writing, articulation, difference – is thus present within language from the very beginning (p. 315/443). This is why language has no pure, simple or unmediated origin.

Conclusion

So, Derrida concludes both his reading of Rousseau, and *Of Grammatology* itself, with perhaps his most powerful articulation of its central theme: what historically goes under the name of 'writing' is at the origin not only of speech, language but of the entire programme of logocentrism. It is this supplement at the origin, an originary state of mediation, that also dooms every attempt to establish a metaphysics of 'presence'. As with all the other terms we have met throughout this book, the originary supplement is, strictly speaking, unthinkable from within the logic of metaphysics: it is neither primary nor secondary, present nor absent, positive nor negative but the interplay of forces that makes all these oppositions possible. To be sure, the deconstruction of metaphysics must continue to borrow all its resources from the very thing it seeks to deconstruct. We have no choice but to employ metaphysical language even if what we are attempting to articulate or designate – *arche*-writing, originary trace or supplementation – is impossible or nonsensical within those terms (p. 314/443). If deconstruction seeks to 'transcend' or 'overcome' the metaphysics of presence – and Derrida himself is notably sceptical of such claims – it must always do so from within, by loosening up its structures, revealing the contingency of its gestures, showing why things need not always be the way it claims they are. In Derrida's own words, deconstruction escapes the metaphysics of presence by nothing more than a 'hairsbreadth' (*une pointe*) (p. 315/443), but arguably the major achievement of the *Grammatology* is to define, map and exist within this vital critical space.

Conclusion: After *Of Grammatology*

In concluding his reading of Rousseau, Derrida also concludes *Of Grammatology* itself. It is entirely typical that this most unusual of books should have no ordinary ending: the text simply stops. On one level, this may simply be an accident of composition: the *Grammatology*, like most of Derrida's books, is a collection of essays on a theme rather than a linear argument that progresses from A to Z. Yet, in a deeper sense, the absence of an ending is very appropriate. To Derrida's way of thinking, as we have seen, *Of Grammatology* is not a book like any other but something that challenges the very idea of a book. What he calls 'writing' is not something that can be limited to the pages of a book with a definite beginning and end, that we can pick up or put down at will. For Derrida, on the contrary, 'writing' consistently exceeds any attempt to define it as a set of fixed empirical marks (like the letters on a page) and constantly spills over into the 'real' world outside the book: we can no longer identify a point at which writing comes to an end. If the *Grammatology* cannot come to a 'natural' conclusion, though, it will still be useful to briefly review what we have learnt from it and, perhaps, more importantly, what we can take away for the future. What, then, has taken place in *Of Grammatology?*

Summary

First, I want to briefly summarise the argument of this text. To start with, Chapter 1 argued that Derrida's entire philosophy is based on the premise that the western philosophical tradition could be described as a metaphysics of presence inasmuch as it identifies a pure point or moment of 'presence' as the supreme value, ground or foundation of knowledge. As we have seen in this chapter, Derrida argues that one of the defining modes of this metaphysics of presence is 'logocentrism'. From Aristotle to Saussure, western philosophy champions speech as the guaranteed means of communicating presence – because it is deemed to be closest to the consciousness of the person speaking – whereas writing introduces a fatal delay, mediation or supplementation into presence. However, Derrida goes on to argue that this logocentric investment in speech falls victim to a basic tension or contradiction that he teases out through a series of close readings of Rousseau, Lévi-Strauss and Saussure. For Derrida, as we went on to see, all language, whether it be spoken or written, is characterised by the essential state of delay, loss or mediation that logocentrism historically assigns to 'writing' alone: language as a whole might properly be described as writing. If the supposed guarantee of presence – speech – is already contaminated with mediation, however, this has important implications for our concept of a pure and unmediated 'presence' itself: what Derrida calls 'writing' is not simply the condition of language because it also describes the field of consciousness, perception and our experience of 'reality' in general. In this sense, what is called 'grammatology' is not merely the science of writing but the science of *everything*: we cannot experience anything in an unmediated way.

Reception History

Second, I want to briefly sketch the reception history of the *Grammatology*. It is hopefully now clear what Derrida's book is about, but the next question that arises is how the *Grammatology* was received by the intellectual community: what contribution did it make to philosophy and to other disciplines? As we have seen, Derrida's work has now acquired canonical status within post-war continental philosophy but in many ways this reputation was slowly and somewhat torturously acquired. To begin with, for instance, Derrida personally, and his work more generally, were welcomed far more readily in departments of literature than of philosophy: deconstruction, indeed, first became known in the anglophone world as a school of literary theory. For Paul de Man, a Belgian émigré literary critic who collaborated with Derrida when the two men were working at Yale University in the 1970s, the *Grammatology*'s forensically close reading of Rousseau provided a new set of answers to traditional questions about authorial intentionality, the role played by the reader in determining meaning and the nature of literary language, meaning and interpretation.[26] In many ways, this literary reading of Derrida's philosophy made sense – he does have a lot of important things to say about authorship, reading, meaning and so on – but it was inevitably somewhat partial in focus and, in lesser hands than de Man's, produced the caricature of deconstruction as a kind of hermeneutic relativism or libertarianism where 'anything goes' in the act of reading.

It was not until the 1980s, though, that anglophone philosophy began to engage with Derrida's thought in a really serious way: deconstruction began to be taken increasingly seriously as a new approach to traditional philosophical areas of enquiry such as logic, ontology, epistemology and – particularly – ethics. As Derrida briefly mentions in the *Grammatology* on a couple of occasions, a key source for his work is the ethical philosophy of Emmanuel Levinas. To Levinas's way of thinking, we only begin to acquire our own sense of subjectivity through a feeling of being indebted or responsible to an 'other [*autrui*]' that exceeds any idea we might have of it.[27] For Derrida, it is clear that the logic of the originary trace has profound ethical implications in the manner proposed by Levinas: the structure of 'the trace', Derrida says in the *Grammatology*, is also the structure of the relation to 'the other' (p. 47/69). To understand the structure of the originary trace, in other words, is to be aware of the constancy of something or someone absolutely 'other' within the order of the 'same'. Every apparently single, autonomous or self-identical element only acquires its identity by reference to some other element that differs from it in space and time. If we translate this logic into more explicitly ethical terms, we gain a radical new vision of our relation to the world around us, to other people and things, to other ways of living, being or thinking. In Derrida's account, we do not pre-exist the other as if we all lived in our own private universes and only later decided to enter the outside world: our own identity, subjectivity or sense of self is originally and essentially constituted by a relation to a potentially infinite number of others.

For Derrida, as we suggested in the introduction, this ethical 'turn' in deconstruction became increasingly pronounced in the 1980s and 1990s with a series of texts that explicitly addressed concrete political topics such as Europe, Apartheid, human rights and immigration. It would be too much to say that he ever constructs a 'politics' of deconstruction but paradoxically this refusal to allow his thought to ossify into a manifesto might be his greatest political contribution. On a deconstructive reading, any political system that seeks to found itself on some moment of pure presence, whether it be the mythical past of conservatism, the 'here and now' of neo-liberalism or the utopian future of communism, inevitably represses the differences, relations and mediations on which it is actually based. To Derrida's eyes, deconstruction's political force lies in its affirmation of an absolute or open-ended future that can never be planned, realised or made present in the form of any political institution, belief system or organisation: 'the unconditional duty of all negotiation . . . would be to let the future have a future [*de laisser de l'avenir à l'avenir*]', he says in a late interview, 'to let or make it come, or in any case to leave the possibility of the future open'.[28] The later Derrida chooses to articulate this position in a quite different vocabulary from that used in the earlier work. This unconditional affirmation of an absolute future begins to be figured in quasi-theological, messianic terms, for example, in texts such as *Specters of Marx* (1994) and *Rogues* (2004). In many ways, though, Derrida's later political thought can, for all its originality, still be seen as a logical extension of what the *Grammatology* says about the originary trace: 'the absolutely other is announced as such – without any simplicity, any identity, any resemblance or continuity – within what is not it' (p. 47/69, translation modified).

What, then, is the reputation of Derrida's *Of Grammatology* today? It is no exaggeration to say that, for better or worse, the text has influenced almost every discipline within the modern academy whether it be anthropology, cultural studies, literature, politics or law. To be sure, Derrida's work continues to be of enormous interest to philosophers. Indeed, the projected publication of almost 40 years worth of seminars will simultaneously cast new light on the *Grammatology* and open entirely new fields of study, apparently including the relation between deconstruction and the concept of life itself. Another key area where Derrida's thought seems more relevant that ever is in the field of technology, media and virtual reality. For Bernard Stiegler, a contemporary philosopher of technology, Derrida's critique of a real, natural or unmediated 'presence' in the name of an originary supplementarity makes possible a new and more radical understanding of the role played by technology in the formation of human life: what is traditionally seen as a mere *tool* or supplement to nature is in fact the *condition* of life, thought and our experience of time.[29] Finally, and perhaps most intriguingly, Derrida's text has also become an invaluable touchstone for philosophers of religion and even theologians. If *Of Grammatology* itself seems somewhat impatient in its attitude to religion – it often portrays the Christian theological tradition in rather monolithic terms as little more than a privileged instance of the metaphysics of presence – philosophers of religion have increasingly forged links between deconstruction and theology. In some ways, Christian theology can itself be seen as a kind of deconstruction *avant la lettre* that seeks to affirm a God who exceeds every concept of being, essence or existence.[30]

The Future

In bringing this guide book to a close, though, I want to go back to the point with which we began: the most important reading of Derrida's *Of Grammatology* is always *the one that is yet to take place*. It is not enough, in other words, to see Derrida's work as merely one more chapter from the history of philosophy that can be digested, learnt by rote and regurgitated in essays and examinations. On the contrary: the text still lies in front of us, waiting to be read as if for the first time. To put it simply, we can never finish reading Derrida's *Of Grammatology* because what is at stake within it is inexhaustible. If everything it tells us about the writing, *différance* and the originary trace is true, in other words, there will always be something more to say, something more to think, something more to read. For Derrida, as we have seen throughout this book, the process of reading, interpreting and perceiving is infinitely open to other, different, future possibilities and nowhere is this more true than in the case of his own work. Perhaps, then, this is the last, most difficult, challenge that Derrida's *Of Grammatology* poses to us as readers and the one that no guide book can help us meet: the challenge to read, think and invent it anew.

Notes

1. Jacques Derrida, 'Letter to a Japanese Friend', in *The Derrida Reader: Between the Blinds*, ed. Peggy Kamuf (New York: Columbia University Press, 1991), p. 272.
2. Geoffrey Bennington, *Interrupting Derrida* (London: Routledge, 2000), p. 11.
3. Aristotle, *On Interpretation*, in Jonathan Barnes (ed.), *The Complete Works of Aristotle: The Revised Oxford Translation* (Princeton, NJ: Princeton University Press, 1984).
4. Martin Heidegger, *Nietzsche*, Volume 4: *Nihilism*, trans. Frank A. Capuzzi, ed. David Farrell Krell (San Francisco: Harper and Row, 1982), p. 164.
5. For Derrida, the chapter entitled 'The End of the Book and the Beginning of Writing' is not advancing a historical or sociological claim about, for example, the decline of oral or print culture and the emergence of new technologies of communication: 'If one does not simply

read the title, it announces precisely that there is no end of the book and no beginning of writing' (*Positions*, p. 13).

6. Richard Rorty, *The Linguistic Turn: Recent Essays in Philosophical Method* (Chicago: University of Chicago Press, 1967).

7. Martin Heidegger, 'Language', in *Poetry, Language, Thought*, trans. Albert Hofstadter (New York: HarperCollins, 1971), pp. 185–208.

8. In his introduction to Derrida, Christopher Johnson draws a suggestive parallel between Derrida's theory of language and the essentially dynamic transmission of information that constitutes both the cybernetic loop and the genetic code. See *Derrida: The Scene of Writing* (London: Phoenix, 1997), p. 46.

9. To be precise, Saussure's argument is that the *general* relation between sound and sense is natural. It is only the secondary matter of which *particular* sound attaches itself to which *particular* sense that is arbitrary. For Derrida, however, the arbitrariness of the relation between every particular sound and sense still disallows any qualitative distinction between 'natural' and 'instituted' signifiers.

10. Saussure justifies his claim that the essence of the signifier is psychic rather than phonic by noting that it is possible to understand the same signifier even when it is pronounced in very different ways (by people with different accents, for example). If we can understand the same signifier even when it is said very differently, this can only be because there is no essential relation between any signifier and any real sound.

11. See *Speech and Phenomena*, pp. 129–60, *Positions*, pp. 8–9 and, particularly, *Margins of Philosophy*, pp. 3–27 for Derrida's most complete definitions of *différance*.

12. For Levinas, the face is the trace of an other who is irreducible to any mode of spatial or temporal presence. See Robert Bernasconi, 'The Trace of Levinas in Derrida', in David Wood and Robert Bernasconi (eds), *Derrida and Différance* (Evanston, IL: Northwestern University Press, 1988), pp. 13–30 for a comparison between Derrida's and Levinas's accounts of the trace.

13. Jean-Jacques Rousseau's second *Discourse* traces the origins of human inequality through a series of stages from the pure state of nature to modern civilisation. It argues that human beings first begin to organise themselves into groups in order to perform specific tasks, but these groups last only as long as the task takes to be completed. At the next stage, we see the development of more permanent social relationships

including traditional family and kinship structures. To Rousseau's eyes, it is this stage – where society has progressed far enough to develop feelings of pity, sympathy and love of others but not so far to become unequal or atomised – that represents the hypothetical ideal society. The next stage in the historical development occurs when the arts of agriculture and metallurgy are discovered because these tasks require a division of labour between those kinds of people who are better suited to physical labour, to the manufacture of tools and to leadership. In Rousseau's view, this stage leads to the creation of social classes, private property and the social and economic inequality that characterises modern society. See Jean-Jacques Rousseau, 'Discourse on the Origin and Foundations of Inequality Among Men', in *The* Discourses *and Other Early Political Writings*, ed. Victor Gourevitch (Cambridge: Cambridge University Press, 1997), pp. 111–231. All further references will be abbreviated in the text.

14. Claude Lévi-Strauss, *Tristes tropiques*, trans. John and Doreen Weightman (New York: Random House, 1977). It is not possible to cite all the evidence Lévi-Strauss gives of the violence of the Nambikwara here but one example will suffice to clinch the point: the anthropologist describes how one day he was approached by a delegation of four tribesmen who asked him to kill another, rival, member of the tribe on their behalf (p. 136).

15. This period, which is broadly dated from 8000 to 4000 BCE, was characterised by a massive expansion in the use of stone tools, the creation of settled villages largely dependent on domesticated plants and animals, and the presence of such crafts as pottery and weaving. As Lévi-Strauss argues, however, all this took place long before the invention of alphabetic script around 4000 BCE.

16. If we consider the inverse claim, for example, the full implausibility of Lévi-Strauss's argument becomes clear: would anyone seriously argue that illiteracy and lawlessness are tantamount to peace and freedom?

17. Jean-Jacques Rousseau, *Confessions*, trans. J. M. Cohen (Harmondsworth: Penguin, 1954), pp. 113–14. All further references will be abbreviated in the text.

18. It is only necessary to cite the following claim among many others where Rousseau equates the pure experience of pleasure with death: 'Enjoyment! [*Jouir!*] If I had ever in my life tasted the delights of love even once in their plenitude, I do not imagine that my frail existence

would have been sufficient for them, I would have been dead in the act' (*Confessions*, p. 210). Translation modified.

19. As Derrida makes clear in a later interview, what he means when he speaks of 'commentary' is not simply a reproduction of the *intended meaning* of the text – this is something that, according to his own theory, can never absolutely be determined – so much as of the dominant *interpretation* of that text: what we might more accurately call the *generally agreed* reading of Rousseau. See Jacques Derrida, 'Afterword: Towards an Ethics of Discussion' in *Limited Inc*, ed. Gerald Graff, trans. Samuel Weber (Evanston, IL: Northwestern University Press, 1988), p. 143. All further references will be abbreviated in the text.

20. To be sure, Derrida's statement is often misread or mistranslated as well as misunderstood. According to Spivak, the phrase reads 'there is nothing outside of the text' but I have chosen to translate Derrida's claim more literally as 'there is no outside-text'. If this translation is more cumbersome, it at least avoids the most misleading implication of Spivak's version, namely, that literally *nothing* exists *except* textuality. In Martin McQuillan's view, the translation of the claim that would be most faithful to what Derrida himself means by it is 'there is nothing text-free': there is nothing, in other words, that is not *also* a text. See Martin McQuillan (ed.), 'Introduction', in *Deconstruction: A Reader* (Edinburgh: Edinburgh University Press, 2000), p. 35.

21. In the helpful interview 'Afterword: Towards an Ethics of Discussion', Derrida argues that what he really means by 'there is no outside-text' is that 'there is nothing outside of context' (p. 136). He goes on to explain: '[w]hat I call "text" implies all the structures called "real", "economic", "historical", socio-institutional, in short: all possible referents. Another way of recalling once again that "there is nothing outside the text" (*il n'y a pas de hors-texte*). This does not mean that all referents are suspended, denied or enclosed in a book, as people have claimed, or have been naïve enough to believe and to have accused me of believing. But it does mean that every referent and all reality has the structure of a differential trace [*d'une trace différentiale*], and that one cannot yield to this "real" except in an interpretative experience' ('Afterword', p. 148).

22. To Derrida's eyes, the relationship between the languages of the south and north is not characterised by a progressive weakening or degradation of values so much as a total transvaluation of those values: what is

'need' in the south is 'passion' in the north, what is 'life' is 'death', 'warmth' is 'coldness' and so on (*Grammatology*, pp. 224–6/319–23).

23. This is why Derrida pays so much attention to the grammar of Rousseau's texts and, in particular, his continuous recourse to what in French is called the conditional tense. As Derrida shows, Rousseau's perpetual insistence on what *could*, *should* or *would* have been the case points to a revealing gap between the real and the ideal, or between fact and value, in the philosopher's narrative (*Grammatology*, pp. 243–4/345–6).

24. For Rousseau, it is possible to identify a stage in the evolution of human language that apparently comes *after* the inarticulate cry of nature but *before* the onset of articulation, convention or supplementarity (*Discourse*, p. 255). In other words, we seem to move from an opposition *between* accent and articulation to a more subtle, if no less problematic, opposition *within* articulation itself (*Grammatology*, pp. 243–4/319–46).

25. In fact, Homer explicitly refers to the very medium that Rousseau claims he is ignorant of in Book 6 of the *Iliad*: Proetus sends Bellerophon to Lycia with a lethal message, inscribed on a folded tablet, which condemns the unwitting bearer to death! The response of Rousseau to this devastating fact is to rather feebly claim that the story of Bellerophon was not composed by Homer himself but was interpolated by later editors (*Discourses*, p. 261).

26. Paul de Man, 'The Rhetoric of Blindness: Jacques Derrida's Reading of Rousseau', in *Blindness and Insight: Essays in the Rhetoric of Contemporary Criticism* (London: Methuen, 1983), pp. 102–41. In the mid-1970s, Paul de Man was an integral member of the so-called 'Yale School' of criticism that sought to apply Derrida's thought to literature.

27. Emmanuel Levinas, *Totality and Infinity: An Essay on Exteriority*, trans. Alphonse Lingis (Pittsburgh, PA: Duquesque University Press, 1969), p. 50.

28. Jacques Derrida and Bernard Stiegler, *Echographies of Television: Filmed Interviews*, trans. Jennifer Bajorek (Cambridge: Polity Press, 2002), p. 85.

29. Bernard Stiegler, *Technics and Time 1: The Fault of Epimetheus*, trans. Richard Beardsworth and George Collins (Stanford, CA: Stanford University Press, 1998).

30. See Arthur Bradley, *Negative Theology and Modern French Philosophy* (London: Routledge, 2004) for a recent discussion of the relationship between deconstruction and theology.

3. Study Aids

Glossary

This section provides brief definitions of key terms in *Of Grammatology*. It is here perhaps, more than anywhere else, that Derrida's work challenges the very idea of a 'philosophy guide book'. To risk stating what will hopefully now be obvious, Derrida's work radically questions the entire philosophy of language on which any 'glossary' is necessarily based: the idea of proper names, of signifiers that relate directly to signifieds, of meanings that can be simply delivered up or made 'present' in themselves. If what follows is not exactly written in bad faith, then, we always need to keep in mind the limitations of this kind of exercise. In a sense, what follows is a perfect example of everything Derrida is talking about in the *Grammatology*: every signifier in this glossary refers, not to an original meaning or signified, but to *other* signifiers in a process that could be extended infinitely.

Arche-writing (*arche-écriture*)

This is arguably the single most important, if still misunderstood term in *Of Grammatology*. It is the principal means by which Derrida deconstructs the logocentric opposition between speech and writing in that text and appears throughout the discussions of Saussure, Lévi-Strauss and Rousseau. Straight away, it is crucial to grasp that *arche*-writing is not the same thing as 'writing' in the everyday or empirical sense of that word: originary writing, as its name suggests, takes place on a more fundamental level than, say, the words on this page. To put it simply, Derrida argues that the term 'writing' names the originary condition of *all* language whether spoken or written. Everything that the logocentric history of philosophy traditionally attributes to 'writing' alone, the mediation of what is supposedly a pure presence actually describes the state of language as a whole. For Derrida, though, *arche*-writing is not simply confined to language because it also describes the mediated nature of perception, consciousness and our experience of 'reality' in general: we think, act and live through signs.

Closure (*clôture*)

This term appears at the very beginning of the *Grammatology* where Derrida draws an important distinction between the notions of 'closure' and 'end' (p. 4/14). On the one hand, he insists that we are now in a position to glimpse the *closure* of the epoch of metaphysics. On the other, he maintains that this does not mean that the epoch of metaphysics is coming to an *end*, indeed, it may continue indefinitely. For Derrida, it is clear that 'closure' signals the conceptual or theoretical *exhaustion* of metaphysics. If we are now in a position to recognise the limitations or finitude of the age of metaphysics, however, it does not mean that we can simply consign metaphysics to the dustbin of history: we have no other language, tradition or system of thought to put in its place. In many ways, then, we might see the concept of 'closure' as a means of responding to what Derrida sees as the defining problem posed by metaphysics: how can we question metaphysical or logocentric ideas, discourse and language while recognising that we have no choice but to continue using them?

Deconstruction (*la déconstruction*)

This term has, for better or worse, become synonymous with Derrida's whole approach to philosophy. It is important to note, though, that the term only appears in very specific contexts in his early work, usually as an allusion to Heidegger's '*destruktion*' of the history of ontology, and nowhere does he suggest that it is the 'proper name' for his thought. As Derrida makes clear on a number of occasions, it is impossible to offer any clear or simple definition of deconstruction but the following points are helpful to bear in mind. First of all, deconstruction is not a philosophical destruction or demolition but an affirmative process that seeks to reconstruct a given system or structure otherwise: it is the 'undoing, decomposing and de-sedimenting of structures' *in order to* 'understand how an "ensemble" was constituted and to reconstruct it to this end' ('Letter to a Japanese Friend', p. 272). Second, deconstruction is not something that Derrida *does* to a metaphysical system or structure from 'outside' – in the way that a surgeon applies a scalpel to a patient's body – so much as something he *reveals about* the way such structures are already internally constituted. If any metaphysical system claims to deliver up a pure or simple 'presence', Derrida demonstrates that it is actually based upon a structural or foundational instability – the network of differences, relations and traces that he variously names *arche*-writing, the trace and *différance*. Finally, then, we might say that what is called 'deconstruction' might best be understood as the basic state or *condition* of any system, structure or network of signification. In this sense, we are in all in a permanent, ongoing state of deconstruction.

Différance

This famous term appears at a number of key points in the *Grammatology*. It is first used in the discussion of Ferdinand de Saussure's differential theory of the linguistic sign. As Derrida makes clearer in other texts, *différance* brings together two different connotations of the French '*différer*': differing and deferring. On the one hand, it signifies the way in which the meaning of any sign is spread out across space in the sense that it necessarily refers to other elements that exist alongside it in the system. On the other, it connotes the way in which the meaning of any sign is deferred or postponed in time in the sense that it always refers to elements that exist before or after it in the linguistic system. For Derrida, language works through this process of perpetual differing/deferring where the task of fulfilling meaning is always devolved onto the next sign along in space and time: we never arrive at a fully present meaning or signified which brings the process to an end. In Derrida's account, *différance* ultimately becomes a means of exposing the originary state of mediation that underlies logocentrism and the metaphysics of presence more generally: every supposedly 'present' element only obtains its identity through differing from, and deferring, other elements that are not simply 'present'.

Double Reading

This important phrase is used by Derrida to describe his own reading methodology in the *Grammatology*. It appears in the important essay entitled 'The Exorbitant: Question of Method' that is appended to the chapter 'That Dangerous Supplement'. On the one hand, a deconstructive reading must seek to *reproduce*, as faithfully and rigorously as possible, what is, or what is generally agreed to be, the author's own intention in writing a text. On the other, a deconstructive reading must also go on to show the ways in which that text *exceeds* or *overtakes* what appears to be its author's own intentions and makes possible new or counter-interpretations. In many ways, Derrida's reading of Rousseau in the *Grammatology* is a model of this double reading strategy.

Logocentrism

This is the term Derrida uses to describe the deep underlying assumptions of the western philosophical tradition from the Ancient Greeks to Heidegger. According to the etymology of the term, 'logocentrism' signifies the philosophical attempt to find the *logos*: a term which can be literally translated as 'word' but also carries within it the larger sense of 'logic', 'reason' or 'meaning'. To Derrida's eyes, however, what really defines logocentrism is that it always privileges speech (*phone*) over writing (*gramme*) as the means by which the presence of the *logos* is expressed: 'the history of truth has always been . . . the debasement of writing and its repression outside "full" speech' (p. 3/12). If logocentrism is so deeply ingrained within western thought and culture that we might think it merely describes 'the way things are', Derrida shows that it is in fact the product of a set of highly problematic assumptions about presence, speech and particularly writing. In the *Grammatology*, Derrida challenges the logocentric attempt to champion speech as the vehicle of the *logos* by arguing that, in a technical sense, *all* language, both spoken or written, might be described as 'writing': writing describes the originary condition of language itself.

The Metaphysics of Presence

This is another key term (along with logocentrism) that Derrida uses to describe the basic assumptions that underlie western thought. According to Derrida, the western philosophical tradition from Plato to the present day dogmatically posits a pure, full and unmediated *presence* as the supreme value. To Derrida's way of thinking, this 'presence' can take many forms: the presence of the subject to itself in thought, sight or touch, the presence of something in space and/or time, even a presence which has now been lost or which may be gained in the future. For Derrida, the metaphysics of presence expresses itself through the institution of a series of binary oppositions and hierarchies whereby a superior term will be identified with pure presence and an inferior term with the mediation or loss of that presence: speech versus writing, nature versus culture, the masculine versus the feminine and so on. In the *Grammatology*, Derrida seeks to deconstruct these binary oppositions by articulating a logic of mediation, difference and deferral that makes them possible in the first place.

The Supplement (*le supplément*)

This is a key term that appears in Derrida's reading of Jean-Jacques Rousseau. It is one of the various ways throughout the *Grammatology* in which Derrida articulates the logic of difference, deferral and mediation that undercuts the metaphysics of presence. According to Derrida, the figure of the supplement performs two irreconcilable roles within Rousseau's text. On the one hand, Rousseau continually presents it as an *addition* to something that is already full, present and sufficient in itself. On the other, Rousseau's text consistently reveals that it is a *substitute*, or compensation for, something that is essentially lacking, insufficient in itself (p. 145/208). For Derrida, then, the logic of the supplement becomes a means of deconstructing Rousseau's logocentric commitment to presence: what should be fully 'present' in itself is revealed to contain an essential lack or absence that always calls for supplementation in the first place. In Derrida's account, we can thus speak of an 'originary' supplement in the same way that we would speak of an originary trace, writing or difference.

The Trace

This is another one of the principal means (along with *difference*, *arche-writing*, and the supplement) by which Derrida seeks to deconstruct the metaphysics of presence. It first appears in the context of Derrida's reading of Ferdinand de Saussure. Adapting Saussure's differential theory of language, Derrida argues that every sign can only obtain meaning in itself by differing in space and time from other signs in the linguistic system. To Derrida's eyes, this means that every sign must originally retain the *traces* of the other signs against which it is to be defined if it is to achieve any meaning at all. For Derrida, however, this 'originary' trace becomes the means for deconstructing not simply Saussure's theory of the sign but the entire edifice of the metaphysics of presence: it re-describes 'the entire field of being [*étant*], which metaphysics has defined as the being-present [*étant-présent*]' (p. 47/69, translation modified). In Derrida's account, every supposedly 'present' element originally and essentially contains the traces of other elements that are supposedly 'absent': nothing, therefore, is ever wholly present or absent.

Writing Under Erasure (*écriture sous rature*)
This is Derrida's name for his occasional rhetorical strategy of crossing out, or holding at arm's length, key terms from the history of philosophy: for example ~~Being~~. It is an approach borrowed from the later Heidegger and appears occasionally in the *Grammatology*. For Heidegger, crossing out terms like ~~Being~~ or ~~is~~ (while still leaving them legible) was a means of clearing away the centuries of metaphysical connotations that had accrued to them and returning to their original, Greek meanings. If Derrida finds Heidegger's strategy still too metaphysical, because it posits a pure or uncontaminated origin that we can return to by clearing away the detritus of history, the process of writing 'under erasure' still provides him with a way around the age-old dilemma of being compelled to use the language of metaphysics when it is that language that he most wishes to question. In other words, writing under erasure enables Derrida to *both* use metaphysical terms like 'Being' *and* mark his resistance to them at the same time.

Further Reading

This section provides a brief selection of key texts in the history of the reception of the *Grammatology*, and of Derrida's thought more generally. To be sure, what follows is not remotely comprehensive: a list of every single text that cited Derrida's work would be considerably longer than this book! In my view, though, the following texts are a useful first port of call that will help to familiarise new readers with the kind of issues, debates and interpretations that are at stake in reading the *Grammatology*.

Spivak, Gaytari Chakravorty, 'Translator's Preface', in Jacques Derrida, *Of Grammatology*, trans., Gayatri Chakravorty Spivak (Baltimore, MD and London: Johns Hopkins University Press, 1976), pp. ix–xc.

In many ways, Gayatri Spivak's massive 'Translator's Preface' to the English edition of the *Grammatology* remains the single most influential commentary upon the text if only because more people seem to have read it than the book it introduces! It goes without saying that Spivak's translation was a massively important event in the history of deconstruction and her own preface does an impressive job of introducing Derrida to the anglophone reader. However, it is possible to commend Spivak's immense achievement while also questioning some of her interpretations. To begin with, Spivak places Derrida in a very specific historical lineage as the latest thinker in an ongoing hermeneutics of suspicion that stretches from Nietzsche to Freud: Derrida's complex engagement with the history of philosophy is somewhat lost. More seriously, as we saw in Chapter 2, there are also some questionable interpretations of the text: Derrida's argument about the 'beginning' of writing is accused of containing a 'slightly embarrassing messianic promise' (p. lxxxi), for example, but this claim does not quite do justice to the philosopher's careful distinction between the 'end' and the 'closure' of metaphysics.

De Man, Paul, 'The Rhetoric of Blindness: Jacques Derrida's Reading of Rousseau', in *Blindness and Insight: Essays in the Rhetoric of Contemporary Criticism* (London: Methuen, 1983), pp. 102–41.

As we saw in the conclusion, Derrida's work was initially welcomed far more readily in departments of literature than of philosophy in the 1970s and 1980s. Paul de Man, a Belgian émigré literary critic who worked at Yale University, was one of the earliest figures in the anglophone world to engage with *Of Grammatology*. De Man's famous essay 'The Rhetoric of Blindness' is a re-reading of Rousseau's *Essay on the Origin of Languages* in the light of Derrida's ground-breaking analysis of that text. However, de Man, while clearly indebted to deconstruction, is not an uncritical follower of Derrida. For de Man, Derrida's 'double reading' of Rousseau – which, as we have seen, continually seeks to reveal unconscious excesses or blind spots within the text – neglects the fact that in a certain sense the text is 'aware' of its own contradictions: 'Rousseau's own texts provide the strongest evidence against his alleged doctrine . . . he "knew" in a sense, that his doctrine disguised his insight into something closely resembling its opposite' (p. 116). In de Man's account, what Derrida calls 'deconstruction' can be seen as a kind of self-reflexive gesture that is proper to literary or figurative language itself.

Jonathan Culler, *On Deconstruction: Theory and Practice after Structuralism* (London: Routledge & Kegan Paul, 1983).

To many observers, Jacques Derrida's work reached a peak of popularity in the anglophone world at the beginning of the 1980s and it quickly became compulsory reading on many undergraduate courses. This text is one of a number of critical works that were written to introduce the key aspects of his thought to a student audience. However, it is striking that the focus is still on the implications of deconstruction for literary criticism – another indication of the somewhat partial reception of Derrida within the humanities at the time. For many readers, Culler provides extremely clear and accessible summaries of Derrida's reading of Saussure, his critique of structuralism and other key aspects of the *Grammatology*.

Christopher Norris, *Derrida* (Cambridge, MA: Harvard University Press, 1987).

Another admirably clear general introduction to Derrida's philosophy. Christopher Norris offers a series of close commentaries on a number of chapters from the *Grammatology* including the readings of Saussure, Lévi-Strauss and Rousseau. Once again, the principal focus is on the 'literary' or linguistic Derrida, though, although there are some gestures in the direction of an 'ethical' Derrida in the final chapter. For Norris, it is important to see Derrida's deconstruction as a direct extension of the Kantian, and more generally Enlightenment, project, as opposed to a critique of it, and this leads him to draw a series of parallels between deconstruction and the analytical tradition in philosophy. In Norris's later works, in particular, this premise leads to some controversial readings not simply of

Derrida but of other movements in contemporary French thought such as postmodernism.

Simon Critchley, *The Ethics of Deconstruction: Derrida and Levinas* (Edinburgh: Edinburgh University Press, 1992).

If Derrida's work was initially received more generously by Anglo-American literary critics, philosophers began to take deconstruction more seriously from the mid-1980s onwards. After the publication of ground-breaking texts by such figures as Rodolphe Gasché (1986), for instance, we begin to see a new interest in Derrida's relation to the history of philosophy (Hegel, Heidegger and Husserl) as well as attempts to apply his thought to traditional areas of philosophical inquiry such as logic, ontology, epistemology and, particularly, ethics. For many readers, Simon Critchley's text is a landmark text in the reception history of Derrida's philosophy because it was the first to explicitly tease out what we have seen to be the ethical implications of deconstruction. The text is largely aimed at an advanced reader with some knowledge of deconstruction but the clear style and argument still makes it very accessible. In general terms, the book is a comparative reading of Derrida and Levinas but there is an excellent early chapter on the relation between the 'end' and the 'closure' in the *Grammatology* and the whole notion of a '*clôtural*' reading.

Geoffrey Bennington and Jacques Derrida, *Jacques Derrida* (Chicago: University of Chicago Press, 1993). Originally published as *Jacques Derrida* (Paris: Seuil, 1991).

For me, this collaborative volume is still the most rigorous introduction to Derrida's philosophy as a whole and essential, if challenging, reading for any student of deconstruction. On the top half of each page, we get a very clear and systematic account of deconstruction written by the Derrida scholar and translator Geoffrey Bennington. On the bottom half, we get a new text by Derrida himself which was expressly written to exceed, surprise or overtake Bennington's attempt to capture his thought within a system. In Bennington's contribution, there is a point-by-point summary of Derrida's reading of Saussure's theory of the sign in the *Grammatology*.

Richard Beardsworth, *Derrida and the Political* (London: Routledge, 1996).

This is another landmark text that teases out the political implications of deconstruction through a series of important, though difficult, close readings. Again, it is not directly aimed at the new reader but the opening chapter offers an excellent re-reading of the *Grammatology* as a political text: Derrida's analyses of Saussure, and particularly Lévi-Strauss, become the basis for a 'politics' of deconstruction that seeks to affirm an absolute or 'messianic' future that exceeds every form of political organisation or institution.

Christopher Johnson, *Derrida: The Scene of Writing* (London: Phoenix, 1997).

This short book is a very clear introduction to Derrida's philosophy. It places his thought in the historical context of the debate between phenomenology and structuralist anthropology. If most introductions try to offer a comprehensive overview, this text consists of a detailed close reading of the chapter on Lévi-Strauss from the *Grammatology*. From this very specific location, the larger implications of Derrida's thought are gradually teased out.

Martin McQuillan (ed.), 'Introduction', in *Deconstruction: A Reader* (Edinburgh: Edinburgh University Press, 2000), pp. 1–46.

This is the place to start for anyone approaching Derrida for the first time and looking for a short overview. It is explicitly written for a student readership and provides admirably lucid and unpretentious accounts of such concepts as *différance*, *arche*-writing and textuality.

Nicholas Royle, *Jacques Derrida*, Routledge Critical Thinkers (London: Routledge, 2002).

In this volume, written by another leading Derrida scholar, we are given a clear, but playfully written, overview of key themes within deconstruction from *Of Grammatology* to the later work, with examples drawn from literary critics. If the book is predominantly written for an undergraduate audience, it is admirably unwilling to 'normalise' Derrida's thought by turning it into just another theory or methodology to be applied and the result is a highly original, quirky and provocative deconstructive event.

Answering Essay and Examination Questions

In this section, we will briefly discuss the kind of essay or examination assignment you are likely to encounter when you study Derrida's work at degree level. What, to begin with, are the most common types of essay or exam questions on Derrida?

1. Exposition: This assignment typically asks you to take a short passage from *Of Grammatology* or other texts and explicate it. This means (a) to lay out in detail the structure, meaning of key terms, and overall sense of the passage; (b) to put it into context with respect to what Derrida is up to more generally; (c) possibly also to contextualise it with respect to other philosophies (structuralism, phenomenology); (d) you may also be asked to assess the *validity* of Derrida's views here.

2. Specific or Historical Philosophy Problems: This assignment asks you to consider Derrida's relation to the history of philosophy, including his debates with, or critiques of, predecessors like Husserl and Heidegger.

3. General Philosophy Problems. This assignment will ask you to use a Derridaean analysis to illuminate a more general philosophical problem, field or area, such as ethics, aesthetics or the philosophy of religion.

4. Application: This assignment is more common in disciplines outside philosophy and will typically ask you to use a Derridaean or deconstructive analysis to illuminate some other kind of text, whether it be a novel, a film, a religious or political tract or a work of architecture.

Common Assessment Criteria

In general terms, your essay or exam answer will be assessed on some or all of the following criteria:

1. The ability to precisely and accurately explain the meaning of a piece of terminology, a passage, an argument or an idea.

2. The ability to philosophically enrich and clarify a particular notion with respect to Derrida's work as a whole, and other philosophies (structuralism, phenomenology).

3. The ability to use secondary commentators. This means showing the ability to (a) find them (through intelligent use of all the resources available to you); (b) digest them (to not get caught out by changes in style or language, and to not get lost in details or irrelevant side-issues); (c) summarise them correctly; and (d) and employ them usefully (to be critical with respect to both primary and secondary writers, rather than assuming they must be right; and allowing their work to inform your own thought rather than substitute for it).

4. The ability to not merely report on the meaning of a bit of philosophy, but to intelligently and fairly assess its merits or truth.

Tips for Writing about Derrida

Finally, we come to the essay or exam answer itself. What is the best way to write about Derrida's philosophy?

1. To start with, you should reference passages in *Of Grammatology* using the style employed in this book, that is, to both the French original and the English translation. In other words, a typical reference should look like this: (*Grammatology*, p. 214/308).

2. It is essential to cross-reference terms that you find in your reading against the original French words. As we've seen, Derrida is difficult, sometimes impossible, to translate and you don't want to make a point in your essay that is based solely upon a weak or tendentious translation. For instance, a key claim like '*il n'y a pas de hors-texte*' is arguably mistranslated by Spivak as 'there is nothing outside of the text' so it wouldn't be a good idea to base your argument upon her interpretation of that statement.

3. As we know, Derrida uses a very specific technical vocabulary. To be sure, key terms like '*arche*-writing' are often very difficult to understand but we have no alternative but to use them ourselves: don't avoid them or substitute some other word in English that strikes you as roughly equivalent. So if you mean '*différance*', say '*différance*'.

4. However, the opposite extreme is also to be avoided: writing *like* Derrida. Unfortunately, quite a lot of Derrida criticism reads like a bad parody of the man himself: we get endless turgid puns, wordplay,

rhetorical questions and so on. If you really want to use Derrida himself as a model, try to emulate the patient reading, attention to detail and clarity of argument of a text like *Speech and Phenomena* or of the Saussure chapter in *Of Grammatology*. Your writing will be more clear and effective if you use Derrida's own technical terms and phrases in the first instance, and *then* try to explain them using your own words, examples, or analogies.

5. So: a good essay is a combination of quotation and analysis. Do not quote Derrida and then move on, as if the quotation were self-explanatory or so convincing that it does not need exposition. If this were true, you wouldn't need to write an essay in the first place! In my view, it is also best to follow a quotation with a sentence or two of commentary: 'what Derrida means when he says "there is no outside-text" is . . .'.

6. Finally, pay particular attention to what the essay or examination question is asking. Is it asking you (i) to explain what Derrida meant by X? (ii) Is it asking you to evaluate the validity of X? Or (iii) is it asking you to try and apply X to another text? See above for the common types of assessment.

Bibliography

Works by Jacques Derrida

Speech and Phenomena and Other Essays on Husserl's Theory of Signs, trans., David Allison (Evanston, IL: Northwestern University, 1973). Originally published as *La voix et la phénomène* (Paris: Presses Universitaires de France, 1967).

Of Grammatology, trans., Gayatri Chakravorty Spivak (Baltimore, MD and London: Johns Hopkins University Press, 1976). Originally published as *De la grammatologie* (Paris: Minuit, 1967).

Writing and Difference, trans., Alan Bass (London: Routledge & Kegan Paul, 1978). Originally published as *L'Écriture et la différence*, Paris: Seuil, 1967.

Edmund Husserl's Origin of Geometry: *An Introduction*, trans., John P. Leavey (Lincoln, NE and London: University of Nebraska Press, 1978). Originally published as *L'origine de la géométrie* (Paris: Presses Universitaires de France, 1962).

Positions, trans., Alan Bass (Chicago: University of Chicago Press, 1981). Originally published as *Positions* (Paris: Minuit, 1972).

Margins of Philosophy, trans., Alan Bass (Chicago: University of Chicago Press, 1982). Originally published as *Marges de la philosophie* (Paris: Minuit, 1972).

Glas, trans., John. P. Leavey, Jr and Richard Rand (Lincoln, NE and London: Nebraska University Press). Originally published as *Glas*, 2 vols (Paris: Denoël/Gonthier, 1974).

Limited Inc, trans., Samuel Weber and Jeffrey Mehlman ed., Gerard Graff (Evanston, IL: Northwestern University Press, 1988).

'Letter to a Japanese Friend', trans., David Wood and Andrew Benjamin, in Peggy Kamuf (ed.), *A Derrida Reader: Between the Blinds* (New York: Columbia University Press, 1991), pp. 269–76. Originally published in *Psyché: Inventions de l'autre* (Paris: Galilée, 1987).

Acts of Literature, ed., Derek Attridge (London and New York: Routledge, 1992).

Specters of Marx: The State of the Debt, the Work of Mourning and the New International, trans., Peggy Kamuf (London: Routledge, 1994). Originally published as *Specters de Marx: L'État de la dette, le travail de deuil et la nouvelle Internationalle* (Paris: Galilée, 1993).

Points . . . Interviews 1974–1994, trans., Peggy Kamuf *et al.* (Stanford: Stanford University Press, 1995). Originally published as *Points de suspension . . .* (Paris: Galilée, 1992).

Echographies of Television: Filmed Interviews, with Bernard Stiegler, trans., Jennifer Bajorek (Cambridge: Polity Press, 2002). Originally published as *Échographies de la télévision* (Paris: Galilée, 1998).

Works by Other Authors

Aristotle, *On Interpretation*, in Jonathan Barnes (ed.), *The Complete Works of Aristotle: The Revised Oxford Translation* (Princeton, NJ: Princeton University Press, 1984).

Beardsworth, Richard, *Derrida and the Political* (London: Routledge, 1996).

Bennington, Geoffrey, *Interrupting Derrida* (London: Routledge, 2000).

Bernasconi, Robert, 'The Trace of Levinas in Derrida', in David Wood and Robert Bernasconi (eds), *Derrida and Différance* (Evanston, IL: Northwestern University Press, 1988), pp. 13–30.

Bradley, Arthur, *Negative Theology and Modern French Philosophy* (London: Routledge, 2004).

Critchley, Simon, *The Ethics of Deconstruction: Derrida and Levinas* (Edinburgh: Edinburgh University Press, 1992).

Culler, Jonathan, *On Deconstruction: Theory and Practice after Structuralism* (London: Routledge & Kegan Paul, 1983).

de Man, Paul, 'The Rhetoric of Blindness: Jacques Derrida's Reading of Rousseau', in *Blindness and Insight: Essays in the Rhetoric of Contemporary Criticism* (London: Methuen, 1983), pp. 102–41.

de Saussure, Ferdinand, *Course in General Linguistics*, trans., Wade Baskin (New York: McGraw-Hill, 1959, 2nd edn 1966).

Descartes, René, *Meditations on First Philosophy*, trans., John Cottingham (Cambridge: Cambridge University Press, 1986).

Freud, Sigmund, 'Beyond the Pleasure Principle' (1920), in *On Metapsychology: The Theory of Psychoanalysis*, ed., Angela Richards, trans., James Strachey, Penguin Freud Library, vol. 11 (Harmondsworth: Penguin, 1991).

Gasché, Rodolphe, *The Tain of the Mirror: Derrida and the Philosophy of Reflection* (Cambridge, MA: Harvard University Press, 1986).

Heidegger, Martin, *Being and Time*, trans., John Macquarrie and Edward Robinson (Oxford: Blackwell, 1962).

—— *Nietzsche*, Vol. 4: *Nihilism*, trans., Frank A. Capuzzi, ed., David Farrell Krell (San Francisco: Harper and Row, 1982).

—— 'Language', in *Poetry, Language, Thought*, trans., Albert Hofstadter (New York: HarperCollins, 1971), pp. 185–208.

Husserl, Edmund, *The Phenomenology of Internal Time Consciousness*, trans., James Churchill (Bloomington, IN: Indiana University Press, 1964).

—— *Logical Investigations*, trans., J. N. Findlay (New York: Humanities Press, 1970).

Johnson, Christopher, *Derrida: The Scene of Writing* (London: Phoenix, 1997).

Levinas, Emmanuel, *Totality and Infinity: An Essay on Exteriority* (trans.) Alphonse Lingis (Pittsburgh, PA: Duquesque University Press, 1969).

Lévi-Strauss, Claude, *The Savage Mind*, trans., John Weightman and Doreen Weightman (London: George Weidenfield and Nicolson, 1967).

—— *Tristes tropiques*, trans., John and Doreen Weightman (New York: Random House, 1977).

Marx, Karl, 'Contribution to the Critique of Hegel's Philosophy of Right', in *On Religion* (Atlanta: Scholars Press, 1993), pp. 41–58.

Marx, Karl and Engels, Friedrich, *The German Ideology* (London: Lawrence & Wishart, 1970).

McQuillan, Martin (ed.), 'Introduction', in *Deconstruction: A Reader* (Edinburgh: Edinburgh University Press, 2000), pp. 1–46.

Nietzsche, Friedrich, *On the Genealogy of Morality*, trans. Maudemarie Clark and Alan J. Swensen (Indianapolis, IN and Cambridge: Hackett, 1998).

Norris, Christopher, *Derrida* (Cambridge, MA: Harvard University Press, 1987).

Rorty, Richard, *The Linguistic Turn: Recent Essays in Philosophical Method* (Chicago: University of Chicago Press, 1967).

Rousseau, Jean-Jacques, *Confessions*, trans., J. M. Cohen (Harmondsworth: Penguin, 1954).

—— 'Discourse on the Origin and Foundations of Inequality Among Men', in *The Discourses and Other Early Political Writings*, ed., Victor Gourevitch (Cambridge: Cambridge University Press, 1997), pp. 111–231.

Rousseau, Jean-Jacques, 'Essay on the Origins of Languages in which something is said about Melody and Musical Imitation', in *The* Discourses *and Other Early Political Writings*, pp. 247–99.

Spivak, Gaytari Chakravorty, 'Translator's Preface', in Jacques Derrida, *Of Grammatology*, trans., Gayatri Chakravorty Spivak (Baltimore, MD and London: Johns Hopkins University Press, 1976), pp. ix–xc.

Stiegler, Bernard, *Technics and Time 1: The Fault of Epimetheus*, trans., Richard Beardsworth and George Collins (Stanford, CA: Stanford University Press, 1998).

Index